Negotiation Skills in the Workplace

Harrogate College Library
(01423) 878213
This book is due for return on or before the last date shown below.

D1637672

Leeds Metropolitan University

17 0244875 2

Negotiation Skills in the Workplace

A Practical Handbook

Larry Cairns

Pluto Press

LONDON • CHICAGO, IL.

27431

First published 1996 by Pluto Press
345 Archway Road, London N6 5AA
and 1436 West Randolph,
Chicago, Illinois 60607, USA

Copyright © Larry Cairns 1996

The right of Larry Cairns to be identified as the author of this
work has been asserted by him in accordance with the
Copyright, Designs and Patents Act 1988.

British Library Cataloguing in Publication Data
A catalogue record for this book is available from the British
Library

ISBN 0 7453 1013 3 hbk

Library of Congress Cataloging in Publication Data
Cairns, Larry, 1939–
    Negotiation skills in the workplace: a practical handbook/
Larry Cairns.
        p.   cm.
    ISBN 0–7453–1013–3
    1. Collective bargaining. 2. Negotiation in business. I. Title.
HD6971.5.C35   1996
302.3—dc20   96–8270
                                                         CIP

Designed and produced for Pluto Press by
Chase Production Services, Chipping Norton, OX7 5QR
Typeset from disk by Stanford DTP Services, Milton Keynes
Printed in the EC by The Ipswich Book Co., Ipswich, Suffolk

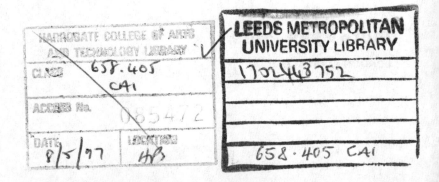

HARROGATE COLLEGE OF ARTS
AND TECHNOLOGY LIBRARY
CLASS 658.405
       CAI
ACCESS No. 085472
DATE 8/5/97   LOCATION HB

LEEDS METROPOLITAN
UNIVERSITY LIBRARY
1702443752

658.405 CAI

Contents

Preface

As a young and less experienced union official I used to try instinctively to review each negotiating experience I had. It was usually a crude affair: I would consider what approach I had taken; what seemed to work; what didn't; and some stab of an analysis at why.

Talking to colleagues, particularly when things were going wrong or progress was sluggish, could be helpful, but not always. They tended to direct their contribution on the subject towards specific aspects they knew best or that had created an impression on them. 'They're always difficult'; 'they don't like the union'; 'the members are weak'; 'they always complain they have no money'. A review was rarely, if ever, a comprehensive analysis and therefore it was deficient as a learning process. Later, when I learned that negotiating was a whole process and not a single skill, I was able to analyse each component part of an interlinking process.

In writing this book I have tried to keep this at the front of my mind in order to offer the reader something more than a cover-to-cover read through, or a dip-into book, but to construct the book in a sequential way which easily permits the kind of review and analysis which will improve the negotiating skills of the reader.

However, whatever motivations my internal struggles to improve my competence as a union negotiator may have given me, I am further motivated by the enormous challenge facing negotiators who represent workers throughout the world, either through trade unions or in some other capacity.

There has been a virtual explosion in the number of players in the business of negotiations throughout the world. Emerging democracies in Central and Eastern Europe are witnessing a rapid programme of privatisation in which wage determination is in a state of upheaval from its historical base. State wage-fixing has to be replaced by Western systems of wage determination. Union activists need to learn the ways of market-based economies and the employers who operate in them. That means learning the skills and strategies of negotiators but in a new and challenging economic and fiscal rationale.

In the reformed democracies of South Africa and other African states, workers and trade unions have been given new rights which need to be channelled constructively lest economic disinvestment is blamed on the workers and the process of reform and progress is set back.

In Britain, as in other parts of Western Europe, the locus and, in certain cases, the economic rationale of negotiations has changed. Privatisation and decentralisation of management decision-making has caused a decentralisation of negotiations. This has propelled many thousands more people into the business of negotiations. Or if they had a role previously, it has become less peripheral perhaps and more crucially tied to outcomes and long-term results.

In municipal government, the National Health Service, and the Civil Service in Britain, various forms of competitive tendering and contracting-out have been introduced which have not only changed the locus and units of negotiations, but the underlying economic rationale. Hospitals have been converted into 7,000 free-standing 'Trusts'. Civil Service departments and functions have been separated into 'agencies'. Schools and further education colleges are now self-managed units with only increasingly tenuous links with their previous masters, the municipal authorities. The current trend in right-wing thinking is that this will make them more responsive to local labour market influences. Industry-wide agreements have, therefore, been undermined and attention has shifted to more localised agreements or to no negotiated collective agreements at all.

Much effort has been put into more 'individually focused' terms of employment. Performance-related-pay and profit-related-pay are the two key innovations. In some cases these are intended to replace fixed and stable components of pay and conditions; in others they are supplementary to them. No reliable estimates exist of the number of people moved from collective agreements to personal reward packages. One indicative fact is that 4,300 managers in British Telecommunications alone now have to negotiate their own annual salary: a job previously carried out by a handful of union negotiators.

In almost inverse proportion to the focus on local markets has been the globalisation of markets and production. Work activity such as data-processing is increasingly being tendered out to parts of South-East Asia with lower labour costs and fewer workers' rights.

The purpose of this book is not to offer a solution to these issues, some of which require political solutions, but to point towards the challenges which face negotiators representing people at work. Collective agreements grow more diverse and ever more complex. These new economic orders pose further challenges to negotiators. It is hoped that this book will permit negotiators not only to develop their skills and strategies in a more methodical manner than in the past, but also occasionally to reflect upon the economic environment within which they function.

Acknowledgements

My thanks for substantial support in writing the law chapter
go to my friend and colleague, John Howard, whose extensive
knowledge of labour law, combined with years of negotiating
experience in trade unions in the UK, make him the most
resourceful person I know in this field.

I would also like to thank Professor John Gennard of
Strathclyde University for allowing me to use his Negotiator's
Aspirations Matrix and for his helpful advice to me in tackling
this project.

Finally, I am grateful to all those colleagues and friends
who shared their experiences with me and provided many of
the illustrative cases contained in this book.

Introduction

This book is for people who negotiate on issues affecting people at work. It is written from the standpoint of negotiators who represent people at work, and primarily it focuses on negotiators who represent people in trade unions. However, the skills and knowledge it covers are transferable into other social, political and semi-leisure activities, and into non-union work environments. The book does not cover business or commercial negotiating where democratic checks and controls are less prevalent, but practitioners in industrial relations, whether in personnel or human resource management, may find valuable insights into the approach, thinking and responsibilities of the negotiators frequently facing them across the table.

The book has been written in a way which takes the reader sequentially through the various stages of the negotiating process. Not every negotiation in which you will become involved will have clearly distinctive stages: some negotiations and the parties to them have well established styles and relationships which make some formalities superfluous. However, the text has been written in this way to help you, the reader, develop a systematic approach to negotiations which can function in a way that is not dependent on any other party's style and approach.

The text also deals with preliminary matters to a negotiation, such as intra-group conflict, the perceptions and attitudes of negotiators, and power as a factor in industrial relations negotiations. It is not essential that the reader work through these initial chapters and you can, if you prefer, jump to the chapter on planning negotiations. However, I would advise you to dip back into these early chapters, as failure to deal effectively with any of the matters discussed can seriously block progress in negotiations.

The book focuses on three primary forms of negotiation:

- Grievance handling, where there is normally scope for pre-negotiation counselling, an opportunity to shape the intended outcome or to obviate the need for negotiations on the grievance by a problem-solving approach which removes the underlying cause of the grievance.
- Integrative negotiations, which contain elements of the joint problem-solving approach, are more open and have an integrity attached to seeking a joint solution.
- Adversarial negotiations, where there are winners and losers and the potential for conflict and imposed sanctions are higher.

The core of the text deals with negotiating skills, but what are these skills? The skills of listening, observing and presentation are perhaps easily understood. Less so, are the tactical skills which are a combination of knowledge and persuasive presentations. A knowledge of economics, industrial sociology, organisational behaviour or psychology may seem helpful, but it is sometimes the synthesis or interaction of factors from these disciplines which a negotiator has to learn to cope with. So there are what may be regarded as single skills, such as listening, and there are composite skills combining an analytical skill, a judgement skill, a tactical skill and a presentation skill. There is, for example, no point in creating setbacks for yourself by making the correct informational analysis and tactical approach and then destroying your position by being over-generous with damaging truths.

Again on tactics, there is a chapter on negotiators and the law. Do not expect this to list or explain helpful areas of employment law. There is not all that much anyway which relates at least to British contemporary workplace issues. This chapter is about the tactical use of the law, the law as a sanction and as a last resort.

Finally, not all negotiations or stages of it are conducted face-to-face. Increasingly, new technology and the pace of life force us to use other forms of communication, so I have offered some advice on negotiations using phones, faxes and letters. For lay negotiators who are perhaps also employees of their negotiating partner, some care has to be taken over how 'open' forms of communication are used.

The negotiating stories or cases I have included are not personal anecdotes but are drawn from a number of sources. To lighten matters and help make the point, a few are laced with some humour which I hope adds to your interest and enjoyment of the book.

I have included some reference to any gender dimension there may be within the negotiating process. Negotiating forums are substantially made up of men, although that is changing – if only slowly. It has been suggested that there are some psychological or cultural differences between female and male negotiators. I know of no convincing academic evidence for this or of any from real life experience. I have, therefore, rejected any such suggestions; if it helps someone else to sell books, so be it! Unlike other representational bodies, the option of 'reserved' places for women negotiators is not a simple option. I have, therefore, suggested various ways in which a better balance of gender and race interests might be achieved in negotiations. The legal obligations placed on negotiators when dealing with equality-related issues is also discussed.

Negotiating is not something you can get absolutely right first time and then think you have mastered it. Whether you mainly deal with one negotiating partner or several, you still have to deal with the perceptions of the other side on different issues and over time. Negotiations at work can range from a personal case which is straightforward and simple to one which is complex and for which a solution escapes you. Collective or group issues can be similar but also put competing and at times contradictory pressures on you as a negotiator.

I hope this text will help you not only to develop a systematic approach to negotiating, by doing a cover-to-cover read through, but also occasionally to review what you have done and dip back into the book and reflect on whether you could improve any aspect of your approach.

A negotiator's job is a lonely one. You usually have people around you brimming with opinions, but when a decision has to be made it is a safe bet that the response to the negotiator will be 'Well, what do you think?' I hope this book will help you to make a skilled and competent response.

1

What are Negotiations?

It has never been simple to arrive at a description of the what, who, where, why, how and when of negotiations at work which is reliable over an extended period of time. The last quarter of the twentieth century particularly has seen the locus of negotiations in industrial relations and the parties involved rapidly changing. The agenda of negotiations has also widened to encompass more issues of interest to workers, but increasingly we have seen employers determining the agenda under the pressure of economic and technological change. Attempts to define negotiations, although they have been made, are of little help to those wishing to improve their knowledge of the process and of only minimal help to those trying to improve their skills in carrying it out.

The term 'collective bargaining' is often used as synonymous with negotiating. This is partly incorrect in the sense that collective bargaining is a more comprehensive term which embraces other exchange processes such as consultation and arbitration as well as negotiations. It may be argued that some forms of worker involvement and participation are contemporary forms of the exchange processes of collective bargaining.

The term collective bargaining has also traditionally been used to embrace the structure of bargaining (that is, the levels, national, district, company, plant etc.), as well as describing the units of bargaining (that is, the occupational groups covered by a single set of negotiations or collective agreement; for example, engineers, fire-fighters, nurses or printers).

The levels at which negotiations take place are usually justified in terms of their economic efficiency. National wage negotiations provided uniformity and stability in wage rates and avoided wage competition and 'leap-frogging'. More localised negotiations, meanwhile, provided the means to reward increased effort, reflect local labour market conditions and permit greater flexibility. Personal or individual contract negotiations have reduced the level of bargaining or negotiations in many thousands of cases in Britain and elsewhere to an individual rather than collective basis.

This latest development has frequently been described as a more appropriate mechanism for rewarding individual merit and performance, while others see it as a political attempt to undermine collectivism. Like many similar schemes of a collective nature in the past, the positive relationship between motivation, performance and rewards in individually focused schemes is at times obscure. Collective incentives – reward schemes that attempt to maintain a close and direct relationship between output and reward based on 'scientific' and systematic measurement of inputs and outputs – have been found to be very costly and difficult to administrate. If we assume that individually focused schemes are more complex to administer, it would seem to follow that they must either be less individualistic than proclaimed or will end up horrifically costly. On the other hand, it can be argued that some occupational groups who could have exploited their strategic or market position in the labour force have in the past had their position constrained by a much larger bargaining unit.

So why should people support higher levels of group or collective negotiations while others seemingly opt for negotiations at lower and more localised levels, even down to individual personal contracts? One reason is that the levels and units of negotiations are not just about the economic efficiency of the process, they are also about the power relationships of the parties. Historically there have been circumstances where employers, trade unions and unorganised workers have shared what they have perceived as a common interest in maintaining negotiations at a specific level.

In the light of more contemporary developments in Britain, Europe and the wider international scene, it is significant that shifting the focus of negotiation to more localised, even individual levels has been essentially a managerial agenda item. In power terms it is difficult to imagine that opting out of collective agreements into personal contracts will, apart from the narrow band of the head-hunted class, have enhanced the power position of such individuals.

TERMINOLOGY

The term 'bargaining' is also frequently used synonymously with 'negotiating' which, in everyday usage, is perhaps accurate. However, to add to the confusion, some people talk about the 'bargaining phase' of the negotiations process. By that they usually mean the concession and exchange stage of across-the-table negotiations. Practitioners can often be heard saying something akin to 'Well, now the preliminaries are out of the way, the bargaining begins'.

In this text I have avoided this distinction as it tends to give that part of the negotiating process greater significance, while I have taken pains to stress that each stage of the process is of equal importance. If, for example, the 'preliminaries' to the actual across-the-table negotiations are done correctly, then the rest may become easier than was earlier anticipated. However, this is not a point to dwell greatly on, and either approach is appropriate for negotiators who in any case usually develop their own natural style of doing things.

PRIMARY TYPES OF NEGOTIATION

As stated earlier, theoretical definitions of negotiations are not of much use to negotiators, but they do need to understand that they are dealing with a process rather than a single event. Negotiations are about regulating parts of the power relationship between people at work and their employer. The process contains the common elements of purposeful persuasion and constructive compromise and a mutually acceptable agreement is normally the intended outcome. Of course, not all negotiations end in agreement and in some circumstances negotiators have to recognise that no agreement can be better than the only deal on offer. Equally, 'constructive compromise' does not mean that of necessity each side has to offer compromise. A negotiator representing a sacked and wrongly accused worker, for instance, wants no less than reinstatement and no blemish on the person's work record. The 'compromise' or 'win' for the employer can be their workers' renewed faith in appeal procedures and fair treatment.

In this text we are focusing on negotiations involving people at work, their unions and employers. Negotiators may have other roles as individuals. This may involve them in negotiations between colleagues over, for example, work allocation. They may be involved in political negotiations within or outwith their job specification. However, here we are dealing with the three primary types of negotiations: grievance handling, integrative negotiations, and adversarial negotiations.

Grievance Handling

Grievance handling is distinguished from the other two approaches listed above because it normally contains opportunities less prevalent in the other two. It can normally be identified as an individual or small-group issue. By virtue of this, there is a more open opportunity for pre-negotiation counselling of members and involving members in deciding the objective of the negotiation. Pre-negotiation counselling in grievance handling can sometimes obviate the need for negotiations.

For example, someone may wish you, as a negotiator, to clarify and re-negotiate their job description or employment contract because they are being repeatedly asked to perform a multiplicity of tasks, beyond contract. The problem, however, may be being caused by bad planning of staff holidays, high labour turnover or poor work organisation. The answer, therefore, may be to deal with the problems rather than try to ring-fence the worker from the symptoms of these problems.

A complaint about low or interrupted earnings in a payment-by-results system may not justify re-negotiating the relationship between pay and output; it may be more appropriate to advise management that poor workflow and work organisation, unless corrected, will have to be compensated for financially.

This form of negotiation, by providing greater scope and flexibility for counselling, advice and involvement, differs from the often 'cold-case' advocacy required of negotiators in other situations where objectives are pre-determined for you. Grievance handling can frequently, but not always, allow you to validate the member's grievance but suggest a different remedy.

In summary, then, the techniques of pre-negotiation counselling and problem-solving can be as successful in grievance handling and personal cases as the direct interface with the employer in more formal negotiations.

Integrative Negotiations

Integrative negotiations are, in plainer language, akin to joint problem-solving in which there is a gain to each side, sometimes referred to nowadays as win–win negotiations. Integrative negotiating is not a style; it is not even always an option for union negotiators. In some issues where there is great financial cost involved for the employer, and gain for the union's members, it is a win–lose situation.

For integrative negotiations to take place there has to be a potential for finding a common interest, a shared recognition that a problem exists and can be resolved by adopting a joint problem-solving approach aimed at finding a new rationale and mutually agreed solution.

Integrative negotiations can be as equally, if not more, stressful for some negotiators as the one-sided assault of adversarial negotiations. You usually find that to solve problems jointly you have to be more open about them. You have to examine a range of possibilities. Why? – because it is still negotiation and you have to ensure that the size of your 'win' is not outweighed by the other side's, while still maintaining your motivation to seek a joint solution.

Adversarial Negotiations

Adversarial negotiations most commonly revolve around the larger economic issues involving higher 'costs' to the employer (namely, wages, holidays, reduced working time, greater income security, equal pay). However, the principle of union recognition and the rights and facilities made available for the union to function are also involved.

In recent times there has been greater potential for a mix of approaches to resolving conflicts of this kind. Technological change and international competitiveness continue to drive a workplace revolution which needs to be regulated and its performance maximised. The negotiated acceptance of change at work, linked to improved pay and rewards, can be beneficial to workers, employers and the industry as a whole. In some issues under negotiation a mix of approaches can be relevant and valuable. For example, a vocational training budget can be a costly item, but negotiation of criteria, selection and training priorities might focus on common and shared interests.

The ability to strike and cause economic hurt to the employer is, of course, another dimension of adversarial negotiations. This ability is dependent on market and economic environments. A worldwide economic recession has substantially dampened exploitation of the strike weapon, as has the changing and uncertain future of particular companies during the last two and a half decades.

These descriptions are not meant to imply that all negotiations are strictly compartmentalised. Sometimes negotiations can contain aspects of the same issue which can be dealt with using different styles and approaches: for example, training budget and selection for training. There may be some aspects of a negotiable item which cause deep conflicting opposition, and other aspects which are of shared and common concern. The purpose of these descriptions is to give negotiators an opportunity to recognise them when they arise and make any choices should the opportunity arise.

SUMMARY

The negotiating process in the workplace is a complex phenomenon involving the practitioner in everything from the disciplines of economics to human and organisational behaviour. To a different degree than other negotiating scenarios, complexity is compounded by the greater significance of the power relationship between the parties and frequently by parties external to the core process such as governments, public opinion and the media.

The level, size and formation of negotiating units do change over time. All over Europe, East and West, we have seen a shift away from national negotiations towards more localised arrangements and to personal contracts inevitably bringing more players into the negotiating processes.

Everyone coming into negotiations should have some knowledge of what they are about, the various stages they will pass through and the skills involved. At a theoretical level, negotiations can involve knowledge of a number of disciplines but a knowledge of these does not make a good negotiator. It is the synthesis and interaction of different factors in each separate negotiation and knowing when, where and how to deploy them which is decisive.

In this chapter I have also referred to three primary types of negotiation. My reason for dividing negotiations up into these three types is twofold: first, to provide you with the opportunity to identify these when they arise and make whatever fine-tuning adjustments to your approach that may be called for; and second, to allow you to reflect on past negotiations and consider whether you might have done something differently, or a different outcome may have been achieved, or the quality of the relationship between you and those on whose behalf you negotiated may have been better.

Finally, negotiations can be messy, untidy and difficult to predict. It can be more like a game of snakes and ladders than computerised chess. Throw the wrong number and you move back a few places. But as we move through the next few chapters we will steadily unravel the 'art' of negotiations.

The following three chapters cover aspects of the negotiating process which are rarely given the importance they call for within the framework of that process. Yet they are elements of the process which, if not handled skilfully, can undermine the most well-prepared case. For this reason, they have been placed sequentially before what may be regarded as the meat of the subject starting in Chapter 5. The three aspects are:

- Attitudes and communication. Attitudinal difficulties coming from your opponent can mean your case can be stifled or completely stonewalled.
- Intra-group or intra-union conflict. This can mean vague objectives and confusing signals are sent to your opponent.
- Power in negotiations. An improper evaluation of your power position can leave your case foundering.

It is to examine these three important aspects of the negotiation process that we now move to in the next three chapters.

2

Attitudes and Communication

In the field of industrial relations stories abound of circumstances in which long-term relations between the parties have been shaped for the good or bad by the attitudes of the key negotiators. Skilful handling of negotiations by union negotiators or, conversely, ineptness when confronted by inherent hostility can significantly influence institutional relations at company or organisational level as well as bargaining outcomes. This dimension of negotiating skill has in recent times become increasingly crucial. Decentralisation of negotiations within industry, commerce and the public sector has brought more participants into the negotiations process from different backgrounds and with attitudes which inevitably impact on the quality of negotiations. The development of additional tiers at a European level poses similar problems. When set alongside continuing intense domestic and international competition in the private sector and its transmission of pressures on to resources in the public sector, these issues have called for a re-assessment of attitudes of all players in industrial relations negotiations.

In this chapter we will look at the factors which influence the disposition of negotiators and then go on to look at how attitudes towards specific values and issues have changed over recent times.

FACTORS SHAPING THE GENERAL ATTITUDES OF
MANAGEMENT NEGOTIATORS IN INDUSTRIAL RELATIONS

For the most part, key negotiators in management will try to reflect the general disposition of the employer, be they national or multinational, public or private sector. However, in *A Behavioural Theory of Labour Negotiations*, Walton and McKersie have shown that the underlying factors shaping their general attitudes to negotiations can be expressed under four headings:

1. the power relationship between the parties as influenced by product and labour market conditions, technology, and the industrial and social legislative framework;
2. the personalities and beliefs of negotiators;
3. the bargaining experiences of negotiators;
4. public opinion.

Defined in broad terms, these factors help to shape the general disposition of industrial relations negotiators towards the negotiating process itself and the direction and influences of that process.

Let us look at factor 1: the power relationship between the parties. Product markets, labour markets and technology are given factors over which union negotiators have no significant overall influence. However, a product market whose cost structure is about to be markedly impacted by technological change in the manufacturing process and the willingness of the labour force to co-operate with that change can affect and change management negotiators attitudes. The union is seen as a threat where previously it may have been regarded as an agent of change.

Similarly with factors 2 and 3: many countries are dependent on inward investment which can mean importation of managerial-level staff. They may have no negotiation experience from which to judge a new relationship. They may resent the 'third party' intervention of a union negotiator. Their personalities and beliefs can have been shaped in an unfettered private capital environment, with no moderating public policy influence. Public opinion can often be fickle, particularly where local economic development is perceived to be threatened.

However, as well as shaping the broad and general disposition of managerial negotiators towards the negotiating process itself, these factors also influence their attitudes towards trade unions themselves. Simply summarised, this can fall in degrees between hostile and co-operative. Hostility ranges from contempt and distrust to grudging acceptance, but normally involves a policy of seeking to limit union influence. Co-operative modes range from one based on mutual respect, a belief in collective bargaining and common interest, to a more collusive and participative relationship. Union negotiators can often take a simple measure of this in terms of the facilities afforded to them to function at the workplace.

In general terms union negotiators know their opposite numbers pretty well and what attitudes they strike towards the process of negotiations. However, in a period of rapid economic, political and technological change it is wise to monitor this periodically to uncover any shift in attitudes towards the union or the reconciling of problems.

Company mergers and takeovers frequently bring with them proposals to alter the product and how labour is utilised. Highly unionised areas of the public sector have had to respond and review their position in the face of competitive tendering out to a highly non-unionised sector in many cases.

It is helpful, therefore, where change of any kind is possible or imminent, to look at the four factors influencing management negotiations and decide whether there is a prospect of change and whether corrective action may be required.

CHANGING ATTITUDES IN THE BRITISH INDUSTRIAL SCENE

Observers of the British industrial relations scene in the late 1970s and 1980s will identify the factors discussed above as influencing the parties in some of the major disputes of these years. This period witnessed successful British miners' strikes in the 1970s, carefully manipulated by miners' leaders under the most favourable market conditions and public opinion and under a more traditional management. In the 1980s and 1990s we saw a new managerial attitude borne out of a belief in management's unfettered right to manage, and a major strike called in much less favourable market conditions and under a new legislative framework that tempered public opinion.

We saw the National Graphical Association locked in a bitter battle with Eddie Shah, in the *Messenger* newspaper dispute over union recognition. Overriding the market technology factors was the social belief of this 'child of Thatcherism' that joint regulation of industrial relations was not a necessary condition. Equally, differences are evident in the newspaper industry where, under similar economic market conditions, some complex industrial relations problems were resolved peacefully, while those involving the personality of Rupert Murdoch were not, and led to prolonged bitterness reminiscent of Ford disputes in the pre-Second World War period.

On the other hand, unions in Britain learned from their disastrous experiences of the 1970s in the public sector disputes. They learned that public opinion must be more carefully considered and managed.

Clearly, in the last quarter of the twentieth century unions in Britain have been disadvantaged by industrial restructuring. The decline of traditionally unionised heavy industries has been succeeded by the growth of electronic and other companies with uncertain product markets and managerial attitudes borne out of the unfettered free enterprise of America's West Coast. On the other hand, many of these companies use the so-called just-in-time production supply systems which make them vulnerable to industrial action and some of them wary of traditional union attitudes and thinking. For many negotiators a new rationale, a new consensus had to be found.

CHANGE, COMMUNICATION AND CONSENSUS

Of course, as well as broad general attitudes, negotiators frequently have attitudes towards specific issues and values. Precedent, the application of the status quo, custom and practice, are all values which have formed deeply entrenched attitudes among union negotiators, while 'management's right to manage' has dominated managerial thinking. In other areas shared values have developed: for example, the 'common rate' for the job, cutting out competition for labour and establishing minimum standards. During the 1970s and in an intensive form since then, product and labour market conditions, technology and social and economic conditions have brought about a workplace revolution which has compelled a re-assessment of previously held attitudes on both sides of the old industrial divide. Some managements have sought to influence the attitudes of union negotiators and workers towards a whole range of changes categorised under human resource management techniques. Equally, social pressures have forced managements to change their attitudes on everything from smoking at work policies to 'core' and peripheral business and employment policies. On the other hand, unions would accuse some management negotiators of still having slothful attitudes towards equality at work and opportunities for continuous vocational training.

Persuasion and negotiation have of course not been the only methods used to bring about change. The bypass technique has been used in which, through inducement or threat, direct appeals have been made to workers, bypassing union channels. This practice brought into sharp focus a management doubt that on certain issues unions could not deliver a sufficient change in attitude to meet new situations.

What is required in these situations is a new 'underlying market rationale' to inform negotiations. If the old rationale of stable prices, moderately consistent technology, a 'known' list of competitors, and stable markets is now gone or going, it is management's job to communicate that. But communications need to start with the what and why of the problem. Attitudes can only be modified if people understand the problem and have adequate testable information about that problem. Giving a quick summary of the problem and shoving a one-sided solution in front of people is neither a democratic nor an efficient way of changing attitudes and devising a new rationale for negotiations.

For unions and management it is important not to completely ignore normal procedures, but a break from the normal channels of communication on both sides can signal the significance of what is to be discussed. Equally, who the message is told to, and who tells it, can be important in grabbing people's attention. Timing is also important. Studies have shown that bringing unions in too early can weaken the credibility of a message. A long time-lapse in which nothing or seemingly contradictory things occur can misleadingly suggest that there was nothing in what was said or that circumstances have changed with no explanation being given.

Where radical change affecting how people work and what they are paid is being proposed, the key to finding a new rationale is not in convincing them of the need for each incremental change. The key is persuading workers and their representatives of the business and commercial necessity for the changes.

In the Timex Scotland 1993 industrial dispute the company failed to sufficiently convince the workers and their union of their transition from an own-product manufacturer to a sub-contractor for other companies' products under international price competition. It might also be said that the trade union set itself a lofty, if not impossible objective: that of obtaining complete reinstatement of all the sacked workforce on unchanged terms and conditions, i.e. the status quo ante. It is hard to think of any areas of employment where, in a radical transitionary stage, negotiators have been able to deliver a solution suitable to everyone. Teachers and policemen take severance or early retirement rather than face learning new tricks after years of dedication to the old ones. When the National Dock Labour Scheme in Britain was abolished, thousands of dockers chose to leave their industry rather than be demoted, as they saw it, to 'general dock workers'.

So, managements should not set objectives for unions which they by themselves could not achieve. Equally, in some situations, unions have to respect the integrity of what they are being told rather than focusing on whether they like the message or not. At the end of the day workers make up their minds on a collective basis but for individual reasons. Some see work as a part of a whole social existence, others, for differing reasons, see that tapering out. Many managements have recognised this and have used the individual contract of employment to get round union collective opposition. Whether that produces more conscripts than volunteers is an open question.

What is clear is that in recent times it has been management, rather than workers and unions, who have been setting the negotiating agenda. However, it cannot be left to them to seek new attitudes and a fresh rationale; union negotiators must at times take the initiative. Simultaneously, workers' and unions' expectations of employers keep growing. They must, therefore, at the very least seem willing to contemplate change if circumvention strategies are not to be the order of the day!

INDIVIDUAL AND INTERPERSONAL ATTITUDES IN NEGOTIATIONS

Most of what has been said in this chapter on attitudes has referred to negotiations within the institutional relationship of employer, employees and unions. Within that kind of institutional relationship, the players, the negotiators, are expected to submerge certain attitudes and beliefs. This is particularly so if they are felt to be potentially damaging to the relationship continuum. For example, a union negotiator may have to choose whether to disclose a personal hatred for tobacco when dealing with a cigarette producer. Health Service union officials may mask a political objection to private health provision if the union has organisational aspirations in that direction.

All negotiators are similarly obliged to mask or totally submerge some attitudes and beliefs. Can you imagine the effect of a Western hostage negotiator talking about the defects he has observed in the theology of Middle East religions to terrorists from that region. I say these things by way of introduction, because there is universal consensus, if not consistency in practice, in this area of negotiating practice. However, in another area of individual and interpersonal attitudes, that of gender and ethnic differences, many people feel that differential attitudes and conduct are seen as permissible.

In Britain negotiating forums are predominantly male and white. Other countries will have their own gender and race or ethnic patterns. There is little academic evidence to prove the existence of sexist or racist conduct in the negotiating process in Britain. This, however, does not prove that it does not exist and internationally negotiators will reach their own conclusions.

A significant amount of anecdotal evidence suggests that women negotiators are likely to have to interface with prevalent, 'masculine' social beliefs and attitudes with which they may not identify. In the experience of the author, where women negotiators experience sexist or seemingly patronising conduct, they would admit that trust and respect take longer to attain. On the other hand, few, if any, would agree that this makes them any less effective as a negotiator. General advice on how to deal with this kind of problem is difficult to give. There is little evidence that women negotiators find it too stubborn a problem in their direct negotiating relationships. Some have been known to turn it to advantage. Ethnic differential conduct by its nature offers no positive opportunities.

Both male and female negotiators have to decide whether attitudes towards them are impeding negotiations, why, and what, if anything, can be done about it. If trust and respect for the integrity of a negotiator's position is absent, then the process is already impeded and attitudes need to be tackled and re-shaped. If conduct is borne out of unconscious but objectionable social attitudes, then a more subtle approach may remedy the situation.

A more contemporary attitudinal problem exists in relation to race and sexual harassment. If the harassed and harasser are both union members, who do union negotiators defend? Thankfully, the Code of Practice on Race Discrimination in Employment (see Appendix B) makes that absolutely clear. The Code on Sex Discrimination (see Appendix A) is less explicit and helpful. Harassment is predominantly, though not exclusively, male on female. It is critical that negotiators get their own attitudes right on this. Of course, proven cases are important but the wrong attitude can help facts to remain concealed. Employers have a duty to stamp out such practices. Union negotiators must, in the interests of the dignity of women and those suffering harassment, be seen to be supporting them.

PERCEPTIONS AND MISPERCEPTIONS

When looking at the four key factors which help shape the general attitudes of negotiators, you would recognise that, apart from the public opinion factor, the rest were historical or given influences whose negative effect, if that be the case, will be difficult to change in the short term. However, most negotiators have a continuous relationship with their opposite numbers and it is possible through example, practice and influence to modify unhelpful or prejudicial attitudes – but patience and persistence are called for. During any negotiation it is open to you to build on what is positive and ensure what is negative is not allowed to cloud your judgement or get in the way of your objective. Individual and interpersonal attitudes, if they have a direct bearing on the negotiating process, are a different matter and some of these have been discussed.

However, another problem area is that prevailing attitudes may be based on perceptions and sometimes misperceptions your opponent has of you or you have of them. It is an everyday truth that first impressions are lasting in your life experiences. You go to buy a car and the salesman or private seller tells you they are looking for £6,500. This figure may be aspirational and their best previous offer might have been as low as £5,500, but if you get it for £5,700 you tell people you saved £800. Why? – because the £6,500 stuck in your mind. Frequently the first thing someone hears about a union or its negotiators sticks and is usually reinforced and difficult to shift.

So it is vitally important at times to clarify your position and that of your opponent. That can mean asking questions or providing a more lucid explanation of your proposals, perhaps with statistics, or by taking the initiative and flagging up possible misperceptions and getting them out of the way first. It may also mean distinguishing your objectives and reasons from others your opponent may have heard. It can also be done formally or informally by simply asking your opponent what they think of your proposal and what concerns they may have. In this way you are seeking to change any impression or misperception they may have of you, or the position you represent.

Negotiations can be a game of bluff, counter-bluff and shielding the truth. It is relatively simple in this environment for misperceptions to arise. The following example illustrates this. Prior to one set of annual wage negotiations, word got out that the company was expressing concern about the level of absenteeism and intended to make cuts in sick pay. Shop floor supervisors reported universal hostility to this and the workforce's intention to mandate their negotiators not even to discuss any such proposals.

The company retreated from their position but made a very low offer on pay which was rejected out of hand. Both sides dug in and the negotiations deadlocked. The company negotiators stated that their hands were tied because senior management were furious at the union's insistence on protecting flagrant and expensive abuses of a comparatively generous sick pay scheme and ignoring the disruptive effect it was having on production flow. The union denied this, accusing the company of using a smokescreen to introduce cuts in sick pay.

The company asked if the union would be willing to look at a presentation of absenteeism patterns. They did, and it revealed excessively high absenteeism at certain times of the year in certain departments. The union asked for an adjournment during which staff representatives acknowledged abuse of the scheme but said they were as flatly opposed to abusive exploitation of the scheme as the company and were willing to discuss how this could be curbed. Sick pay rates were guaranteed but a joint review of the rules was set up, and a satisfactory agreement on pay reached.

SUMMARY

Paying attention to the disposition and attitude of your opponent in negotiations is important in that it helps you to view things from the alternative viewpoint. It is more crucial in a changing environment than in a stable one, but it is a constant factor. Dealing with this can range from defusing individual resentment to adopting a long-term process of pressure, persuasion and emphasis on positive and consensus items to get matters looked at in a new light.

Management negotiators need to appreciate that union negotiators or employee representatives do not have the same access to management information systems as they have.

Even where information is shared, it is better to start with the problem than the solution and the relevance and weight of information are as important as the facts themselves.

Union and employee negotiators dealing with new and contentious areas in negotiation can profitably spend some time thinking through how to cultivate the most positive attitude in the other side before getting down to the meat of the issue. In the field of sex and race discrimination and harassment, continuous diligence is required – negotiators must be seen to be firmly on the side of the harassed.

Judging and influencing attitudes in negotiations is essentially a preliminary part of the process but can be vital to a successful outcome. For a fuller account of tactical suggestions for modifying negative attitudes see Walton and McKersie, *A Behavioural Theory of Labour Relations*.

3

Resolving Intra-Group Conflict

This chapter sets in context the issue of intra-union and intra-group conflict. These are the conflicts and disagreements which inevitably occur within your own side over objectives, tactics, the negotiator's approach, the progress being made, the timing, and so forth. Successfully reconciling these differences is crucial to the progress and outcome of any negotiation. Here again there is no rigid set of rules but this chapter provides the tools and approaches which can be used to reach consensus, if that is at all possible.

The chapter also introduces the issue of gender orientation of demands and equality and the impact that can have on intra-group conflict. At the end of the chapter a number of case studies are set out which help to illustrate that intra-group conflict can arise at a number of levels in negotiations and that the consequences can override all other considerations in the negotiating process.

It would be surprising if, within a process involving different interests, positions and politics, conflicts did not arise. Add to this the inverse hierarchy of most representational structures such as trade unions where power resides at the bottom among individuals, and it becomes ever clearer why conflict arises and why that conflict and its resolution through intra-group bargaining has become an essential part of negotiations at work. This holds just as true in non-union environments where it may be even more difficult to obtain a sustainable consensus on certain issues.

This part of the negotiating process does not form part of the formal negotiations. It takes place outside the particular negotiation – offstage so to speak. It is a sub-process which can take place within a group, a union, or between unions, between negotiators and their members, or a negotiator and the union hierarchy. It can occur before the real negotiations begin, at settlement stage, or be almost a continuous undercurrent shadowing the whole process. Some examples are given later in this chapter to illustrate some of these points. Equally, it can be seen from these and other examples that the resolution of intra-group conflict can be decisive in terms of the efficiency and shape of the final negotiated outcome. For that reason the role of the negotiator in this part of the negotiating process is a crucial one.

THE DUAL ROLE OF THE NEGOTIATOR

Clearly, during all but the most exceptional negotiations intra-group conflicts do arise, but what is the relationship between these intra-group conflicts and negotiators? Next to outcomes, such conflicts should be seen as the single most important experience influencing the quality of the relations between negotiators, the parties they directly represent, and others involved in intra-group conflict surrounding negotiations.

The negotiator has a central role in resolving such internal conflicts. This role is one of counsellor and adviser to those s/he is representing. The negotiator therefore has dual roles in the process of negotiation: first, as a negotiator confronting the employer and prosecuting the workers' claim, and second, as a counsellor/adviser to the individual or group on whose behalf they are acting.

The counsellor/adviser role can, on occasions, be a much misunderstood one. It is one in which union negotiators frequently feel a conflict between their two roles and must therefore be fully understood if they are to achieve competence and confidence in their role. The counsellor/adviser role of the negotiator can be required on at least four formal stages of the negotiating process:

- at the stage of claim or grievance formation;
- during adjournments in the negotiating process;
- during interim report-back stages;
- during final settlement recommendation stages.

However, those you represent frequently see each of these stages as democratic opportunities to mandate or constrain their negotiators. On the other hand, the negotiator may foresee difficulties in prosecuting a particular claim, be experiencing setbacks during negotiations, or conclude that the gap between people's aspirations and what is on offer is unbridgeable. Bearing these factors in mind, the two most common approaches or styles open to the negotiator are:

- a passive approach in which claims, grievances, report-backs, final offers are taken up or given without comment or evaluation;
- an active interventionist approach which involves a 'leader' approach to counselling and advising members perhaps to raise their aspirations, 'stick to their guns', defend the union's interests, or conversely counselling individuals to moderate what they are asking closer to what is thought negotiable, giving a balanced and neutral critique of what has been offered at various stages of negotiations, weighing up the pros and cons of an offer, and suggesting that individuals or groups may have to modify their aspiration to achieve a settlement.

In some circumstances negotiators may employ a less defined and more mixed approach. This can be simply a matter of emphasis and degree. For example, a negotiator can accept a claim as being in the form of a mandate but draw members' attention to the limitations of it or of the optimism it radiates.

The question of whether a union negotiator takes a passive or interventionist approach to the resolution of intra-group conflict may be determined by the degree of control or influence they can reasonably exert. For example, wage or salary claims may be determined by a democratic process in which the negotiators themselves are not directly involved or have minimal influence, and any intervention may be limited to the latter stages of the process.

SOME TACTICAL CONSIDERATIONS IN INTRA-UNION BARGAINING

Just to repeat the point, intra-group conflict is one of the most important factors impacting on the quality of relationships between negotiators and those they represent. However, in one sense this sub-process is not bargaining or negotiating at all. As a lead negotiator you are not negotiating with the group at all in the commonly accepted sense. You are not striking a deal with the union or its members or other representatives. You are not even an equal partner. Whether your partners in this interaction are individual members or the union executive, power in this context is almost one-sided. The nature and purpose of this interaction is, however, different from the formal negotiations. There is an exchange taking place. Information is being exchanged, pressures applied, power levers pulled, but the focus of this part of the process is on seeking a new rationale, a fresh and renewed authority, a new mandate. The means by which this is done is through the exercise and deployment of the few powers available to union negotiators in this context. These powers, however, are not executive and devolved from above. They are less tangible, they derive from the status and legitimacy of negotiators, the knowledge they hold and the expertise they employ.

Legitimacy

Negotiators need to assert their status as a lead-partner in a negotiation with the exclusive responsibilities which that carries. If management are to be expected to respect and recognise the status of a union negotiator, then they will only do so knowing they are reciprocating something already afforded by the union or group. Power emanating from status is therefore one lever in the armoury of union negotiators.

Equally, the legitimacy of information, advice and counselling flowing from negotiators is another form of power. Negotiators are the legitimate authority for articulating the views, claims, assertions and arguments of those they represent when confronting management. If the legitimacy, weight, and authority of that articulation is to be recognised and respected by management, then the power of its legitimacy must also be recognised by the union and its members. Of equal reciprocity is the legitimate responsibility placed on negotiators to articulate the degree of determination on the part of the members to pursue or indeed the employer's determination to resist any particular claim. Ignoring, undermining, or even misreading the legitimacy powers of negotiators in this regard can be a costly mistake.

Knowledge

The powers deriving from knowledge and expertise are most likely to be the ones having a negative impact on the quality of the relationship between negotiators and other parts of the union during intra-group conflict. It should be recalled that negotiations are a process to regulate part of a power relationship, and that the resolution of intra-group conflict is an integral part of that process. It is perhaps natural in that context, that knowledge and information forming part of and flowing from that process are frequently regarded as one-sided and treated with suspicion. The quality of relationships between negotiators and those they represent can mistakenly turn on the negotiator being seen as the broker of two or more conflicting views or perceptions, and thereby being manipulative.

There is little that can be done to avoid these pressures and tensions completely – it is the nature of things, and, as they say, 'it comes with the ticket'. However, some expertise can be employed to reduce the stresses of these situations. Firstly, some judgement has to be made about what you communicate and to whom. Reporting seriously every expression of shock, horror and disgust made by management can injure your credibility at best, at worst it can sound as if you are leading up to explaining failure. Equally, communicating every dire threat you hear from either side can heighten resistance or undermine your credibility if it does not happen.

Negotiators can also reduce the charge of sounding manipulative by involving other members of the team or by filtering reports through other representatives. On occasions written reports or bulletins have more legitimacy than oral ones. For small-sized meetings and interactions flip-charts can add a useful visual dimension to a report. Deciding what, when, where and how to communicate all form part of the legitimate armoury and power of negotiators in the resolution of intra-group conflict.

EQUALITY AND INTRA-GROUP CONFLICT

Pressure to give a higher priority to equality bargaining issues can impose conflicting intra-group pressures on union negotiators. There are expectations among people at work that women negotiators will influence the bargaining agenda and prioritise issues of most interest to women. On the other hand, women negotiators, particularly professional officers, see part of their role as balancing the interests of all members, regardless of gender.

Having said that, women negotiators, few as there are, have succeeded in broadening the bargaining agenda. They have brought a fresh focus and impetus to the cut and thrust of intra-group conflict in favour of women members. Many have defused the competing strains of gender politics by pointing out that negotiable items such as maternity leave can extend to paternity leave, and so on, thus embracing the interests of both genders.

Widening the negotiating agenda has also brought added tensions to intra-group conflict. The equality agenda now extends beyond simple equal rights issues within a basic legal context. It now includes items designed to bring greater social as well as employment equality, and as such stimulates more intense debate on social priorities in this area. Additionally, lobbying by interest groups to have their interests prioritised can sometimes put pressures on negotiators when the aggregate cost of settlement is worked out.

However, the belief that harnessing the frequently amorphous constituency of women at work will in itself lead to gender solidarity on all equality issues does not match with reality. Women, like men, want a say in the shape, content and priority of certain issues. The age profile in a workplace can determine whether 'family leave time' is a bigger priority than improved childcare payments; just as most older and childless employees may be less sharply attracted towards matching workplace holidays with school holidays than younger working parents.

In many areas there is for negotiators almost a fusion of the interests of gender and of race. In both areas industrial relations negotiators have identical responsibilities. They must not aid or abet direct or indirect discrimination, whether the pressure to do so comes from the employer or employees. More positively, union negotiators have a policy responsibility to promote equality of gender and race.

INTRA-GROUP EXCHANGES

A unified demand has more impact and tactical advantage than one where people are divided and self-interest is the dominant theme. So even where there is no spokesperson or negotiator whose responsibility it is to reconcile individual or conflicting views, then informal exchanges during work breaks or after work can help to produce a more cohesive and unified view, opinion or demand.

For example, settling holiday times, new working hours or shift patterns may require consultation with partners or other family members. Rash decisions based on a particularly vocal or domineering viewpoint could result in unfair pressure or serious consequences for individuals, perhaps forcing them into giving up their employment.

Discrimination on the grounds of sex or race is another key area in which intra-group exchanges can be essential. Few individuals have the confidence to make their minds up straight off that they have a case for claiming discrimination. Whether discrimination or unfair treatment took place will turn not simply on the law but on the facts of the case. Those facts will invariably involve what other people said or did, how others were dealt with in similar circumstances. So group reactions, though not necessarily consensus, should be sought in such cases.

In the case of alleged sexual or racial harassment, obtaining peer opinions can be crucial. If the case goes to law, witnesses to the behaviour being complained of should contribute clear-cut evidence. There is no benefit in someone harbouring an undeclared personal resentment waiting for their 'day in court'. They may find their colleagues have been unaware or insufficiently sensitive to their predicament. More damagingly, the colleagues may hold the view that the complainant's own conduct failed to make clear that the alleged behaviour was unwelcome. As stated above, total consensus is unnecessary but it helps if others are on your side and share your view of events.

So even where no union exists, workers can help themselves by seeking facts and information through discussion and exchanges of opinions, and thus forming a more solid and unified view to put forward.

On more complex issues relating to pay and conditions, pensions, health and safety, what other people are paid, and so forth, information can be sought from a number of different sources. In Britain, the Advisory, Conciliation and Arbitration Service (ACAS) has offices in most major cities. The Citizens' Advice Bureaux increasingly handle employment questions. Unions, even where they have no negotiating arrangements with particular employers, are willing to help individuals as much as they can.

EMPLOYERS AND INTRA-GROUP CONFLICT

Employers generally take the view that unions, like their own organisations, are pluralistic and may take some time to sort themselves out. Internal union or group differences may impact on the employer and the conflict may become intra-organisational. It would, however, be wrong to assume that their patience is endless. Intra-organisational conflict is a trait in industrial relations recognised by employers and is catered for. Eternal differences within or between unions is not an accepted condition of their union recognition or negotiating rights. For negotiating purposes in times of stability this may not matter; in times of change and turmoil it can be crucial. Managerial frames of reference permit pluralism, but if consensus is not efficiently arrived at, executive authority may decide.

Viewed from this standpoint, unresolved intra-organisational conflict that perhaps impedes industrial relations progress may, in some quarters, be considered an unaffordable luxury. This view has certainly encouraged the move towards single-table bargaining in multi-union establishments and single-union recognition deals in others, most notably among inward investment companies.

SUMMARY

Intra-group conflict is an inevitable ingredient of the negotiation process. It is part of the search for a constructive compromise. People at work rightly regard this as a democratic process in which they have a right to participate and make their views known directly or through their representatives.

Experience teaches negotiators that there are no fixed sets of circumstances which can determine the best approach to intra-group conflict. Neither is it wise for negotiators to limit themselves to a single approach in resolving it. It may be necessary to be leading and urging at the outset and moderating or passive at the final stages, or indeed vice versa. There are no set rules for this and some negotiators will argue that 'intervention' or 'passivity' is a matter of personal style, disposition or choice.

The twin principles involved in intra-group conflict are to guide people towards what will be perceived as the most successful outcome without breaking faith with the group or its wider interests, or undermining your integrity with your opposite number. At its more complex level, negotiators recognise that some demands are more inspirational than expectational. Equally, the interests of everyone in a group are not homogeneous and a management proposal equally applied to everyone may have an unequal and damaging effect on some. It is these factors and many others which give rise to intra-group conflict as part of the process of reaching a satisfactory agreement. Negotiators have a dual and pivotal role in that process – if admittedly at times an uncomfortable one.

The following four case studies illustrate some of the issues in intra-group conflict and the means by which they can be resolved.

Case Study: Bargaining Through Impasse

A large section of teachers were engaged in a long-running dispute with their employers over pay. Their 'industrial action' amounted to little more than 'administrative sanctions' which, while extremely irritating, were not bringing the employers to the negotiating table, let alone to their knees. Quite the reverse, the employers had noticed that despite fairly provocative behaviour on their part, the union side seemed unable to take stronger action.

The dilemma for the union was that:

1. the employer's last offer had been rejected by the union's executive committee controlling the dispute;
2. the employers, sensing union weakness, were publicly putting pressure on the union by calling for a ballot on their last offer;
3. the militants on the executive were strongly opposed to a ballot and urging stronger action; the moderates were equally cool towards a ballot, fearing it would split the union with a damaging split vote on an inadequate offer;
4. the union negotiators recognised stalemate and pressed for some new initiative which would get negotiations going again.

The negotiators decided to inform the executive of the union that without the prospects of a 'show of strength' from the members, any improved offer would be marginal, and that teasing out a significantly improved offer would have to be tied to an assurance to the employer side that the union would ballot on the new offer.

The militants claimed this could lead to a sell-out. The moderates neutralised this by adding a rider that any ballot would not necessarily carry an executive recommendation of acceptance. The negotiators went back to the negotiating table with a new position. The employers had other pressing problems and were anxious to settle.

The employers offered a small improvement on their current offer, coupled to an interim offer on the following year's salary round. The offer went to ballot. The employers publicised the average retroactive pay entitlement during the ballot and 75 per cent voted in favour.

Case Study: Differentials

A large engineering company had been met by the national officers of their general union representing their semi and unskilled workers to state that successive State incomes policies had had a disproportionate and depressive impact on their members' pay. As a result, the policy of the union was to press strongly for flat-rate money increases as opposed to percentage increases which favoured the higher paid.

The employer responded by saying that they were aware of the problem and now that they were free of incomes policy restrictions they would bear it in mind when working out their response to the 'substantial wage increase' claim now being put forward by the Plant Joint Shop Stewards Committee.

The company decided that with the return of free collective bargaining expectations were running high, and the best approach would be a high as possible 'first and last' offer: that is, a single offer which excludes any further negotiation. Bearing in mind what the general unions' officials had said, but without taking soundings from their craft unions, the company offered an £8 per week across the board increase – well above the rate of inflation.

The semi and unskilled workers hailed the offer as highly satisfactory and a victory for union policy. The craft workers were appalled that the company had taken unilateral action to depress differentials which many craft workers felt were too narrow in the first place. The craft workers seriously threatened strike action. The semi and unskilled workers countered this threat with the promise that they would strike if the company altered the flat-rate principle and gave the skilled workers more.

The company responded by saying that if either group struck there would be immediate lay-offs of the other group without pay.

Having said that, there was now an inquiry to find the managerial architect (scapegoat) of this calamitous situation.

The senior shop steward covering all grades, realising he and the company were between a rock and a hard place, called together the Joint Shop Stewards Committee. Before meeting them, the senior steward, a wily character of not inconsiderable experience, asked for an informal meeting with the company to 'clarify the offer'. At this meeting he asked if it was possible that he had 'misunderstood' the company's offer. Was it not the case that the flat-rate of £8 was to be applied to everyone but in the case of payment-by-results workers, exclusively craft workers, this would be added to bonus rates and not their hourly rate, thereby yielding on average a much higher increase than the £8 originally offered?

After a short informal adjournment at which the company negotiators assessed the cost of a strike against the cost of 'recognising there had been a misunderstanding', the company conceded the flat-rate increase would apply to the bonus rates of skilled workers.

After a difficult meeting of the Joint Shop Stewards Committee, a strike was avoided and a consensus reached which included an assurance that the Shop Stewards Committee would support any semi or unskilled group who wished to switch to payment-by-results: an offer never taken up.

Case Study: Cross-Border Bargaining

Without doubt the most celebrated case involving this dimension of bargaining occurred in 1984 between the International Union of the United Auto Workers in the USA, the United Auto Workers (Canadian Section) and General Motors (Canada). The bargaining processes, the partners involved and the levels at which it took place went beyond a direct form of intra-union conflict to intra-organisational conflict involving both the UAW and GM at different levels and at times it appeared at cross purposes.

The issue at stake was whether the UAW (Canada) would permit GM to introduce a profit-sharing scheme that excluded annual hourly rate increases in pay into Canada as they were about to do in the US, through an agreement with the UAW (International).

GM had just announced the biggest profits in its history. The most senior directors had just awarded themselves salary increases of 100–150 per cent. But they claimed competition was stiff and US labour costs were too high and hence annual pay increases had to be eliminated and replaced by wait-and-see lump-sum profit bonuses. UAW (Canada), through its Director, claimed that labour costs were lower in Canada and in any case such a deal was not ratifiable by the UAW membership in Canada. The Director espoused the view that he would rather go down fighting GM than get torn to shreds by the membership for proposing a deal of this sort. For this he had solid backing from his officials in Canada.

On the opening day of negotiations in Toronto, the chief negotiator for GM (Canada), proposed the new wage and benefits package covering a three-year period. As anticipated by the Canadians it was almost identical to the US deal – profit-sharing and no hourly rate increases. UAW's lead Canadian negotiator brusquely and summarily rejected the offer warning that unless there was a fundamental shift in the direction of the negotiations, they were heading for a strike. This view was endorsed by his negotiating committee representing GM plants all over Canada.

Following this, the UAW (International) based in Detroit became involved through its President. He was about to put his signature to the US deal involving profit-sharing claiming that if it was good enough for the US car workers it was good enough for the Canadians. In any case, the US side of the union had not simply acquiesced to profit-sharing, many US plants were on short-time working, and there was a lot of unemployment among car workers, with more threatened.

To make the profit-sharing, no-hourly rate increase scheme more attractive, GM had given assurances about greater job security. The Canadian union responded saying that while they had every sympathy with the plight of American car workers, all Canadian plants were working full time and they didn't have that kind of problem.

With the strike imminent, the Canadian union team were given a stern message from the GM Chairman that he was not intervening in the dispute and that Canadian plants were now under threat and would be axed if the profit-sharing deal was not accepted and a strike ensued. Hard on the heels of that came a warning from the UAW President that authorisation for the strike and access to the UAW $50m strike fund may have to be withdrawn if profit-sharing was the only issue. If there was a strike in Canada, GM plants in the US would be laid off. Because of component interdependency, Ford plants would also be closed within three days. Simultaneously, the lead negotiator was faced with illegal wildcat strikes in some of the GM Canadian plants. This he reckoned would play straight into the hands of GM and the reluctant UAW in Detroit.

He demanded the plants get into line. He realised that he could not fight GM and his own union simultaneously. Revocation of their strike and access to strike funds would mean accepting a profit-sharing deal. He had to make peace with the UAW International. Locked in a Toronto hotel with his team, he engaged in telephone negotiations with the UAW President, finally offering a presentational fudge that would disguise hourly rate increases. The international union President offered to use his good offices to secure a deal on the Canadian's terms and now negotiate directly with the GM Chairman. The GM Canadian chief negotiator was now also cut out.

Three days into the strike the UAW President contacted the Canadians to say the best he could do was a variation on the US profit-sharing deal and the Canadians should consider accepting it. To the Canadians it seemed like treachery. Still encased in their hotel and their strategy in tatters, the Canadians turned back to GM's Canadian negotiator. He then agreed to negotiate a deal embracing the Canadian principles. The lead negotiator advised his team that going down this road spelled the end of the international union. Intra-union negotiations would finish and breakaway would be on the agenda. However, the re-involvement of GM's Canadian negotiator turned out to be another false dawn.

With his original strategy in shreds, the union negotiator still felt his team and all the plants were behind him and decided to up the stakes. He then advised GM and the UAW (International) that the issue was one of principle, the strike would be locked in and GM, US workers and the Canadians would suffer casualties, but they would not give in. In addition, they would not return for minor 'nickels and dimes' concessions.

After eight days of the strike, GM appeared to cave in but warned that if the Canadian workers wanted the principle of annual hourly increases, then there was a price for that and that was low hourly increases. GM scrapped their profit-sharing scheme for Canada, and offered hourly rate increases. The final offer fell short of the team's aspirations but, accepting principles have their price, the final offer was ratified by 75 per cent of UAW Canadian members. Twelve days after the strike began it was over. Six weeks after that talks were initiated to sever the institutional links between the Canadian and US sections of the UAW. This did not occur, but institutional tension remains to this day. Subsequently General Motors expanded its operation in Canada.

Case Study: Municipal Programming

A brusque high-profile Director of Education in a large municipal education authority was faced with a salary claim from teaching unions which his budget could not withstand. Instead, he decided to make his knowledge of the union work to his advantage.

He had made almost as generous an offer as circumstances would allow, keeping very little in reserve to achieve final settlement. Two crucial union executive meetings were due to take place: the first to hear a report from the negotiations; the second to decide on a strategy following soundings from among members. His experience told him that the union's executive was split 50–50 into militants and moderates and his offer was sufficiently on the low side for the moderates to be swayed into sanctions by the militants in support of a higher offer. Since agreement was beyond hope, he decided on a high-risk strategy to sew confusion and prevent unity. Two days before the union executive meetings he released highly provocative statements to the press accusing the executive of being irresponsible, of threatening their own members' jobs, of opposing reasonable and progressive reform in education and not acting in the interests of their members.

The tactic worked. At each subsequent executive meeting the majority of the time was taken up with heated and emotional outbursts and the framing of retaliatory press releases with insufficient time spent on working out a sound tactical response to the offer. 'Shoot the messenger' was the rhetoric, a strain that ran through a series of unproductive meetings laced with unrealistic demands. Over a couple of lengthy meetings, the Director retracted his allegations, conceded that unions in teaching should be given greater scope within consultative structures to air their views on reform in education and made a marginal improvement in the money offer which scraped home at the executive ratification meeting.

4

Power in Negotiations

The first consideration of a trade union negotiator before taking up an individual or collective case for negotiation is to assess the broad, relative merits of the case in question. The second is an assessment of the relative power position of the relevant parties, i.e. member(s) and employer. Most experienced negotiators have been in the position of having a strong case and little power to exert, and less frequently a weak case and power dominance. But what is bargaining power? This chapter does not set out to provide an academic or conclusive definition of bargaining power. It is difficult to see how that would help the practitioner in any case. A more practical approach is to look at some key components of what is termed 'bargaining power' and their relevance and value in negotiations.

In broad and general terms there are four components which make up power in the context of union/management negotiation:

- economic power;
- the power of public opinion;
- power of argument and persuasion;
- the level of determination and organisational ability to pursue the issue.

The reader should not conclude that these are listed in any form of importance or priority. The reason why will become evident later.

ECONOMIC POWER

The economic power of trade unions in the negotiating context is frequently exaggerated and in Britain many politicians consider it synonymous with confrontation and greed. Similarly the press portray union power in almost exclusively negative terms. Perhaps unions themselves willingly accept the myths accompanying exaggeration and insufficiently promote the positive sides of union economic power.

During the 1970s and 1980s much was heard about the monopoly power of trade unions and little of the socio-economic value of trade unions in the workplace revolution of that double decade, nor of the positive advantages flowing to employers from the equality agenda of trade unions in relation to the labour market attraction and retention of women workers. There are, therefore, positive economic advantages that are often neglected in case presentation. These have more ably been promoted in the field of equality bargaining, in which the provision of maternity/child/family leave with pay has been argued in the wider context of labour attraction and retention. New pay and grading structures have made labour flexibility a more practical possibility. Shorter and more varied patterns of working hours have also had socio-economic benefits.

Trade unions are also an invaluable conduit for information about wages and conditions external to the workplace. There can be frequent cries that the grass is greener elsewhere. Trade unions can act as a stabilising influence in this context by supplying more factual and reliable information about pay and conditions elsewhere. Uninformed or misinformed workers can be disadvantageous to non-union employers who might turn up on a Monday morning to find some of their key personnel have gone elsewhere with unrealistic expectations.

Economic Power in the Bargaining Context

In the bargaining context, economic power is a somewhat slippery concept. Its common usage relates to the potential which exists for the trade unions acting collectively to cause economic hurt to the employer. The aim in such cases must be 'hurt' not mortal damage which is reciprocal. In any case, trade unions' intentions are always to maintain sufficiently civilised 'rules of engagement' and to ensure that long-term relationships are retained. The reader will, no doubt, know of an exception!

In this context power relates to the

- elasticity of supply and demand for the product or service;
- the employer's market position;
- the length of the employer's production or service run;
- the availability of alternative labour or production.

An Engineering Union District Committee once coined the oft-quoted phrase: 'when Chrysler wants cars, we screw them and when they don't want cars, they screw us' – wonderfully graphic and helpful exposition of a power relationship, which some may deem out-dated.

In the newspaper industry in the days of 'old technology', unions were reckoned to be powerful. Because of the shortness of the production run and the proximity of the customer, the effect of even minimal sanctions caused an immediate loss of revenue to the employer. 'You can't sell today's papers tomorrow' was the phrase. New technology, the ability to switch production to other plants, combined with restrictive union legislation, has moderated union power in that industry.

In shipbuilding and heavy engineering and manufacturing, with long production lead times, the impact of sanctions was less immediate. In these industries timing and tactics were important if power was to be maximised. According to the trade you were in or your place in the sequence of production systems, you struck when it would have its most inconvenient and disruptive impact. Frequently this would be offset by the employer laying the rest of the workforce off without pay. Equalising the pressures, it was called!

Equally moderating but different forces apply in the railway industry. The impact of strikes in the passenger railways causes an immediate loss of revenue. People who would have travelled today either don't or find an alternative to rail. The moderating influence is the social disruption and public distaste and hostility, most commonly directed at railway workers and their union.

Conversely, miners normally enjoyed general public sympathy and support. In the 1970s in the UK they carefully built upon that and also ensured that strikes took place when coal stocks were low but domestic supplies were guaranteed (thus minimising any public hostility). In 1984 miners were propelled into a dispute during the summer and after a long period of overtime working when coal stocks were piled high. In addition, alternative fuels for electricity generation and managerial ingenuity in distributing power around the grid offset the economic impact of the strike. Even grim determination and wide public support could not counter-balance those factors.

The wrong tactics similarly blunted the economic hurt caused in the road haulage dispute in 1978. In this instance a very determined and well-organised nationwide group of road haulage drivers went on strike. Unfortunately they became obsessed with the 1970s phenomena of picketing. They very effectively ensured that all the goods they normally delivered remained in the warehouses and stockholdings all over Britain. In took some weeks for them to realise that since their employers were only haulage contractors they were not depriving them of revenue and profit, they were simply delaying it, since, apart from perishables, the goods they had picketed would eventually need to be delivered and paid for. As soon as the pickets were taken off and other company or rogue contractors started to deliver the previously picketed goods, the Haulage Contractors Association asked for immediate talks.

In the clothing industry production cycles are short. The production time for a garment can be under half an hour. Production runs are generally short with finished goods in retail shops within two or three days of manufacture. In addition to these factors the industry is labour-intensive with a high dependability on female labour. Such an economic production system may at first sight suggest high employer vulnerability and high economic bargaining power. However, other economic factors are at play in the clothing industry. Clothing is not simply very price sensitive, it is also affected by more underlying conditions of demand than any other product. Fashion, the weather, the general economic conditions and outlook, and politics all play a part. Because of these market factors the industry is comprised of a very large number of small

LEEDS METROPOLITAN UNIVERSITY LIBRARY

to medium-size plants which provide many retail outlets with alternative sources of supply. This example serves to illustrate how the power advantage offered by the econ-production system can be moderated by the economic elasticity of the product and the availability of alternative sources of supply.

These illustrations are offered as evidence that the determination of economic power in the negotiating context is far from an exact science. Its pure form is equally dependent on how, when and where it is tactically deployed. Mistakes can be costly as these real life examples illustrate. It is vital that negotiators have sufficient information to allow them to weigh up the pros and cons of power factors in negotiations and come to some judgement about them.

Other Environmental Power Factors

Other key environmental power factors impacted on negotiating forums during the 1980s and early 1990s. From 1979 the UK witnessed almost unrelenting economic stagnation and high unemployment. The latter part of this period also saw economic restructuring and rationalisation throughout Europe in response to the legislative programme associated with the creation of a Single European Market.

These economic factors combined to have a depressive effect on bargaining outcomes. However, negotiators also saw a return to free collective bargaining under the Conservative government. No norms, no restrictive incomes policies or legislation. Government rhetoric about 'people pricing themselves out of jobs' did of course remain, but had relatively little impact on the negotiating partners.

A more directly targeted government initiative was a conveyor belt programme of legislation designed to tilt the power balance more firmly in favour of employers. They did this by making certain sanctions unlawful, making the placing of sanctions administratively draconian for unions, lubricating the legal machinery of injunctions for employers and introducing unlimited fines on unions for breaches.

Qualified majority voting introduced within the Council of Ministers of the European Union in 1989 brought some minor positive individual rights for workers. While welcomed by unions in Britain, they had no significant effect on the collective influence of trade unions themselves.

Of greater significance to trade union negotiators was the so-called workplace revolution – changes in technology, production systems, work organisation and patterns of work. This, combined with the decentralisation of bargaining, was accompanied by a pendulum swing back from the dominance of production management to personnel and human resource management.

Just-in-time (JIT) production and service systems, Total Quality Management and 'core and peripheral' business organisation touched the private and public sectors equally, bringing 'people management' and negotiating back into focus and extending it to lower levels of employment hierarchies. One example which helps explain this shift in priorities occurred in 1988 when Ford workers in Britain struck and JIT and component interdependency caused the rest of Ford Europe to be laid off within three working days. More traditional systems would have had stock buffers and taken weeks to impact. This experience prompted a mutual re-assessment of sanction strategies on the part of both sides.

PUBLIC OPINION

Public opinion, by its very nature, is a two-edged sword, but with one edge sharper than the other. When it is against you a hostile media will whip it up, and can cause it to be decisive in a dispute. But by itself it does not guarantee the outcome it supports. However, when it is for you it adds to the power behind your case.

Negotiations are not news, breakdowns are. Union negotiators then have to be prepared to explain to the public what they are asking for, how eminently reasonable and justified their members are in asking for it, and how they are not responsible for the breakdown and are willing to return to the negotiating table any time.

Shaping public opinion in this way serves four purposes:

- it helps to offset or neutralise adverse opinion or propaganda from other sources;

- it can bring pressure on the other side;
- it can bolster the commitment and morale of your own members;
- it can temper or neutralise opposition of 'silent partners' in a dispute.

In serving all of these purposes it should be borne in mind that public opinion can be as important in a small local dispute as in large set-piece national confrontations. Analysing the expectation of public opinion has to be a further skill in the armoury of negotiators. It is not the purpose of this chapter to extensively develop how this should be done, but a few examples will illustrate varying degress of success in engaging public opinion to the union side.

In the 1970s, the National Union of Mineworkers built upon the natural level of sympathy the public had for miners by introducing what for many were obscure and complex national wage league tables. These purported to show that miners had slipped back relative to other workers and what the public had said they should have in a previous dispute some years earlier. This took place against the background of government restraint on incomes and yet the NUM skilfully massaged public opinion behind it by the clarity of its exposition on miners' relative earnings. Doing this helped to shift the government position.

During the 1984/85 miners' dispute over pit closures, the strong confrontational nature of the dispute left public opinion more divided. Equally, there was less clarity in the 1984/85 dispute about what would resolve the pit closure issue and therefore there was no distinguishable objective for public opinion to marshall around. Of course the miners' opponents, government ministers and newspapers, were also hard at work manipulating the power of public opinion, equating violence and arrests with guilt. In fact few miners were found guilty of anything.

In disputes involving Health Service staff, public opinion has been skilfully used to evoke sympathy and positive support.

In both of these examples, public opinion has been used to shift the direct negotiating partners, i.e. the Coal Board and NHS management, but also the 'silent partner' of central government.

One last point: it should be borne in mind that the exercise of power can be moderated at times, imperceptibly even to the principals and participants, by an almost subliminal wish to avoid fracturing long-term relationships.

POWER OF ARGUMENT AND PERSUASION

When two or more parties come together for negotiations, for the most part there already exists a consensus that there is something to negotiate about and what that something is. The parties, therefore, come together motivated towards reaching an agreement.

The mistake made all too frequently is to assume from this that the logic and equity of an issue are also already equally apparent to the other side, that includes the front-line negotiators and other senior management. The second mistaken assumption is that argument and persuasion can play a poor second to power politics. If the logic, equity and power of your argument are not already known and developed with clarity before you invoke power politics, you may find it quickly dissipated.

Two positive examples: for public sector unions in the 1980s, the depressive economic environment was compounded by the hostility of central government towards the public sector. Against this background, the unions launched a wage claim in 1985, the centrepiece of which was the assertion that local authority workers were not only low-paid but had considerably slipped back in the national earnings 'league table'. So powerful were the arguments in favour of these low-paid people that, despite tight financial curbs and penalising legislation, the employers shied away from the harsh light of continued public exposure on poverty pay. Central government did likewise.

Similarly, unions, spurred by their women members, recognised the need to shift equality issues off the political agenda onto the negotiating agenda. In the course of this, powerful negotiating arguments increasingly replaced the politics of equality and many more favourable agreements were concluded.

THE LEVEL OF DETERMINATION AND ORGANISATIONAL ABILITY TO PURSUE ISSUES

Bargaining power is also influenced by the level of determination of the parties to pursue issues. For trade union negotiators, this means not simply attitudinal determination but the organisational ability to pursue. A senior union official counselled his members and fledgeling shop stewards thus: 'when I am sitting opposite management in a negotiating session they may be listening to me, but they are looking over my shoulder watching you. If they don't see determination in you they will stop listening to me!' Put another way, he said: I pursue serious union claims, I don't run errands!

Of course, determination should never be confused with blind obduracy. Determination in a negotiating sense has a positive objective. It is determination to obtain an agreement. That implies a determination to address the criteria for reaching agreement or at least seeking to establish one while the potential remains.

Determination itself has a number of tactical dimensions. Persistence and pressure in negotiations can have the effect of wearing down your negotiating opponent. The use of time is another: the continuous recurrence of an issue, perhaps until the time and tide are more favourable, is a wiser deployment of determination than pressing on the same point for a short-term response.

Sanctions as a manifestation of determination were discussed earlier, although there can be special difficulties for negotiators in this area. Determination to continue sanctions may not equate with determination to reach an agreement. On occasions the potential for agreement is so remote that the sanctions become almost an end in themselves. Sit-ins/work-ins in some instances appear to take on that appearance as workers struggle to hold on to their jobs and unions struggle to finance them. In some of these situations the employer often has folded his tent and gone. No negotiating partner remains and the potential for agreement is non-existent.

Who could argue that in the 1984/85 miners' strike there was anything other than grit determination, but organisational ability to pursue demands was flawed by only a partial strike and eventually the NUM preferred no agreement to one they saw as being on the employers' terms.

These examples often suffered from somewhat similar impediments: that is, of strong and inflexible public rhetoric by both sides, strengthening their commitment to a fixed position. Of course, commitment to that becomes personal and corporate pride, loss of face and frequently disaster!

Conversely, what other tactical options are open to union negotiators who find themselves with a strong case but weak or impaired collective determination and an unyielding management? All is not always completely lost. One additional tactical option is to use the law, where relevant, as a sanction. This, however, will be covered in a later chapter in which this approach can be discussed in the depth it justifies.

One concluding comment on this section on bargaining power: it is dangerous to generalise from a single or what seems a comparable example. Power in bargaining flows from a number of sources in various strengths and proportions. This chapter has sought to identify these sources. Their existence, potency and reliability in any given situation is a matter of analytical skill and judgement.

'A powerful argument is always better than a powerful friend if you can never get him on the phone' is often a useful trade union maxim.

SUMMARY

Power is a complex factor in negotiations and the balance can change during the process and therefore has to be monitored. Self-delusion about their power position can be a negotiator's greatest weakness. More often than not, negotiators have an exaggerated view of their power position and that is alright if it is part of a conscious bluff, but can be deadly if it is part of a self or collective delusion. It means corrective action is not taken to offset any weakening in the position, whether tactical or otherwise.

The purpose of this chapter has been to set down in broad and general terms the key components of power in collective bargaining and encourage you to use them in a structured way to assess your position. Are your arguments gaining ground and credibility? Is the determination to pursue the issue being maintained? Has the economic position remained the same or shifted for or against you? If you have applied sanctions, are they working? The same technology used in a different way can reduce the impact of sanctions. Witness to that was the way in which, in the 1984/85 British miners' strike, electricity loadings were moved around the British grid system. In the British Rail signal workers dispute in 1994 computerised signalling systems were used imaginatively by managers to gain 50 per cent train movements during an almost 100 per cent strike. During both these disputes public opinion favoured the strikers for long periods.

Movement in these factors during negotiations can determine whether tactical change is called for, or whether to press home an advantage or reach for a quick settlement. The overall lesson is that your power position needs to be assessed at the beginning and reviewed throughout the period of negotiation.

Case Study: Royal Power

In the city of Seville in Spain in 1995 the hotel waiters and bar staff of the city threatened strike action over a long-standing grievance on pay and hours. The action was timed to take place during the day of Spain's first royal wedding since becoming a democracy. Dignitaries, wedding guests, tourists and royal wedding watchers were arriving from all over the world.

The dispute received worldwide media attention. The Mayor of Seville promised negotiation up until the royal couple walked down the aisle. Visitors to the city and royal event, hotel and restaurant owners, became distinctly nervous about the strike's impact and pressurised the mayor. Ultimately, the dispute was settled just in time for the city and its thousands of visitors to celebrate the royal event. Union officials had already declined their invitation to attend the ceremony!

5

Planning for Negotiations

The previous chapters have essentially dealt with the key background and underlying factors in negotiations. It is now time to move on to the practical elements of the process. This chapter covers three aspects of the planning of negotiations.

- Are you in a position to negotiate? Has the other side agreed that there is a matter which has been legitimised for negotiation? If not, what has to be done?
- Has the negotiating team been selected and have members' roles been determined? The team needs to be briefed on what is at issue, what the objectives are and, most importantly, establishing that there is no dissent on these.
- Are the conditions and arrangements for the negotiation suitable?

ARE YOU IN A 'NEGOTIATING POSITION'?

The concept of a 'negotiating position' is difficult to get to grips with and in particular situations is open to different conclusions. However, it is important that it is understood, otherwise you can spend a frustrating amount of time banging your head against the wall and making no progress. Sometimes a change of approach or longer-term view of the problem may pay off.

Negotiation is a means of joint regulation. It implies a consensus between the parties in each negotiation that there is a matter to be resolved between them using the process of negotiation. If this consensus does not exist then the union is not in a 'negotiating position', and is doing no more than exchanging views. This may be an important stage of the

50

process. It may be educative, exploratory; it might highlight a minority group problem; it may simply be pressurising the other side to think more seriously about the issue – but that then needs to be converted into a willingness to negotiate on the issue.

An everyday example is of a customer buying goods at a stall in a local market and haggling successfully with a willing seller/stallholder over the price. When the same customer moves up the road to Marks and Spencer, any attempt to haggle over prices will be met with a blank stare. The stallholder will be an owner with authority to negotiate prices. The manager of Marks and Spencer has no such authority and the customer is not therefore in a negotiating position.

In industrial relations, a lack of consensus can arise from a number of sources:

1. Lack of authority to negotiate on the item due to constraints being placed on management by more senior management or corporate policy, or other external forces. In the late 1950s and early 1960s employers' associations in Britain tried to hold back the tide of pressure on member companies to agree to 'plant-bargaining' over wages by threatening to expel member companies who conceded higher pay rates at plant level. The once powerful British Engineering Employers' Federation coerced major companies to hold the line until the countervailing pressure of strikes and a realisation that local flexibility on pay rates offered advantages to the employer as well prevailed.

2. Constraints being placed on management because of unequal conditions across the employment locations of their workforce. In the National Health Service the employers were seriously resistant to a standard agreement covering all employees on issues such as childcare facilities and leave time. However, they were willing to concede and agree to the principles on which these were based. Unions, therefore, negotiated the principles and contained them in a national 'enabling agreement', leaving the details to be negotiated at local level according to local preference.

3. Constraints being placed on employers by legislation. It was not uncommon in the 1970s to hear some employers and

unions deciding jointly in a redundancy situation that part-time workers should be sacked first. Until that is, it was pointed out that part-time workers were usually women and the practice was discriminatory and illegal.

Consensus about an issue for negotiation can, however, be absent for reasons of power relationships, economic and/or political: that is, that one partner to the negotiation has become weaker or stronger. This change may be due to changing product or labour market conditions. It may also be due to changed political conditions.

In the late 1980s supermarket chains and many others dependent for labour on school leavers refused to respond to union claims that young trainees should be paid more than the minimum rates laid down by government, claiming they could not afford it. Young people felt trapped by high unemployment levels. In the early 1990s employers changed their position and awarded dramatic improvements in the terms and conditions of trainees. What strengthened the unions' arguments were the changing demographic trends being reported indicating a continuing decline in the number of young people coming on to the labour market. In partnership with their young members, unions articulated these pressures. Some of the demographic projections were subsequently revised.

In 1984/85 the National Union of Mineworkers (NUM) was on strike over British Coal's pit closure programme. It was probably the longest and bitterest dispute in the history of British trade unionism and yet it ended the way it began with no consensus about what was to be negotiated. The NUM wanted to negotiate a criterion for pit closures which was part economic and part political: that is, a criterion which recognised the economics of declining coal reserves and higher costs of coal extraction but also implied the continuation of some form of state subsidy. British Coal, for their part, felt that a single status economic criterion was the only option open to them, a position which was being underlined to them by the Conservative government fully committed to ending state subsidy.

The power relationship between the two sides and the exercise of that power over a 12-month period was unable to shift either British Coal or the NUM towards a consensus about the issue for negotiation. As history tells, the dispute ended in stalemate with no agreed solution. History also tells that British Coal then imposed their economic criterion in the manner and scale predicted by the NUM to add to the folklore of British and international trade unionism.

One major craft union in the UK adopted a wages policy that its members working in manufacturing industry must be exclusively the higher-paid craft manual workers in any plant. Recognising that such a policy was liable to meet with considerable resistance, not only from management, but from other craft workers, it sought to shift the power relationship considerably in its favour by making available its very substantial strike fund to any members striking in support of the union's wages policy.

The union had some minor successes with this policy until it took on Rolls-Royce Ltd. This company had a sophisticated industrial relations management and a well-organised and militant Shop Stewards Committee. There existed a mutually agreed modern wages structure in which all craft workers were on the same top grade.

The union concerned was unable to persuasively articulate why that should be changed to favour their members exclusively. Neither management nor the Shop Stewards Committee were convinced. The craft union had, therefore, no consensus for negotiation. This they intended to shift through the exercise of power and withdrew their labour for 16 weeks. However, an equally countervailing power in management's mind was the likelihood of an endemic consequential strike situation by other groups; a view which was confirmed by the Shop Stewards Committee. With the union's power advantage effectively neutralised, they were back to a no-consensus situation and a deficit in persuasive argument. This case illustrates how failure to get into a negotiating position can at times be due to a failure on the part of the union to communicate the advantages of having a new agreement.

A major plant in Scotland manufacturing clothing and textiles suffered from poor attendance, low earnings, and low morale. Each year at the annual wage negotiations the union complained about low earnings; the management blamed low output and poor attendance records. The union responded each year by tabling a claim for a good-timekeeping bonus and improved piecework times. The company responded by stating it was not company policy to reward people simply for turning up on time and that piecework times were adequate. The claim was, therefore, repeatedly and summarily rejected.

A change of shop stewards and full-time union officer prompted a review of the situation. The review revealed that piecework values were on par with other factories with much higher earnings, but piecework earnings were being undermined by the imbalance in production flow which, in turn, was seriously affected by absenteeism levels, thus providing a disincentive to turn up for work. The union re-presented its claim to management in the form of an attendance bonus linked to output and piecework performance. The union also placed heavy emphasis on the potential value of such an agreement to the company. The company scrapped its principled opposition and agreed to negotiate. In later years the agreement was hailed as a successful innovation.

Employers also have constraints put upon what they can impose. These tend to be greater in unionised than in non-unionised workplaces. Even so, non-unionised workplaces with low levels of worker protection can suffer the repetitive additional costs of higher labour turnover and its impact on quality, reliability, training and staff competence.

Successive British Conservative governments have urged employers to introduce measures permitting what they euphemistically called 'greater flexibility' in settling pay and conditions at work. In essence, flexibility frequently meant lower pay, less stable pay, and the ability to demand longer hours with no increase in pay or shorter hours with pay cuts. Various legal adjustments put employers in Britain in a stronger negotiating position in relation to their workers. The unthinkable became the permissable in the treatment of some sections of the labour force.

REACHING FOR CONSENSUS

The two means to be used to achieve the consensus which will put you in a negotiating position are the exercise of persuasion and power. At an early stage in any negotiator's career it is forcibly brought home that persuasion and power are, in the industrial relations arena, inextricably linked. However, knowing that in itself is simply knowing the raw facts. The skilled negotiator has to know when the deployment of 'powerful argument' will serve better than the threat of economic sanctions through industrial action.

The deployment of argument, as powerful as felt necessary, must, by the very nature of industrial relations, be the first essential of a negotiator's armoury. Threats of industrial action, no matter how veiled, can send signals that you are spoiling for a fight and no matter what is offered, your members are going to have one. Threats may simply find your members on strike with neither side being totally clear as to why they are there or what will get them back. Managerial strategy in these circumstances can be to make no offers at all until the situation cools or make tactical offers in such fine gradations that the threat becomes more expensive to the union than management.

The importance of persuasive argument in the negotiating process is often undervalued. Strikes, as the manifestation of power, are more dramatic, seem more clear-cut and seem to provide winners and losers, but they are often not the most practical or efficient approach.

One single example of this, although there are many others, in contemporary trade unionism, is that unions increasingly find themselves negotiating what are termed in Europe 'social clauses' which are of benefit only to some members in certain circumstances. Issues such as 'career breaks' or 'carers' paid leave' in many workplaces or industries have no natural or stable constituency through which to harness action. Apart from the organisational difficulties, there is also the contemporary legal problem of organising strike ballots at disaggregated membership levels. So on certain issues, increasingly ones of membership priority, union scope to express power is limited.

There is also a second and related reason why persuasive argument can be more efficient and preferable in seeking consensus to negotiate. It is that some aspects of contemporary collective agreements are becoming more complex. There needs to be an educative as well as communicative purpose to the union case.

Agreements on issues such as childcare facilities or carers' leave may raise moral questions, or require a knowledge of state or municipal provision and responsibilities, taxation rules, and so forth. These are matters for negotiation which go on top of the complexity of costing such agreements and defining the status of those who will benefit.

Use of Sanctions and Consensus

If there is no consensus and the union has been unsuccessful in persuading the employer to negotiate meaningfully, then sanctions may be the only legitimate response open. However, in these circumstances it is a hazardous route in which the costs and benefits and likelihood of success need to be weighed.

In recent times the most frequent occurrence of this is in strikes over union recognition. In circumstances where a union has gained sufficient membership in a workplace to justify claiming representation and negotiating rights from the employer, it will feel pressured to gain these rights or lose the members. If the employer is being obstinate or using delaying tactics, the union will feel it has little to lose by calling a strike. Employers, on the other hand, may obstruct union efforts by harassing and undermining the union's organisation, or may decide to compete with the union's aspirations by offering its employees improved terms and conditions.

In disputes involving substantive issues, such as the cost of a pit closure programme, as in the miners strike of 1984/85, the employer will be making decisions about the short and long-term costs of negotiating a settlement or alternatively toughing it out.

In both types of circumstances, however, it is in the union's interest that as much discussion, if not real negotiation, has taken place to determine as precisely as possible what differences there are between the two sides, what reasons lie behind the employer's position, and in the light of these, what the union thinks it would take to resolve the dispute. Even where the exercise of power is necessary for a union to gain a negotiating position, the application and deployment of negotiating skills are still essential prerequisites.

Being in a negotiating position therefore implies two things: first, that both sides recognise that there is a matter that legitimately requires joint agreement between the two parties; and second, that the willingness and authorisation exists to use the negotiating process to resolve the outstanding matter. Establishing a negotiating position may involve persuasion or power. Reasons for refusing to negotiate on the part of the union or management may be overt or hidden and testing them out is a sensible precaution before invoking sanctions.

THE NEGOTIATING TEAM

It is normally advised that negotiating teams should be an uneven number and preferably three. However, trade union negotiators often have little choice about either the size or composition of a negotiating team. It is frequently laid down constitutionally or forms part of a procedural agreement.

Uneven numbers are helpful but not essential. They help to smooth the path if interim decisions are hastily required. Large negotiating teams allow for more group representation and can lead to a broader base of support when it comes to ratifying the outcome of negotiations. On the other hand, large teams can be cumbersome, difficult to keep in control, and often lead to conflicting pressures on the lead negotiator. Large negotiating teams can also lead to problems of confidentiality on negotiating strategy and potentially can make concessions more difficult to obtain. The only general guidance in democratic union organisation over negotiating team size and composition is: as small as possible, and as large as absolutely necessary.

The Core Negotiating Team

Whatever their size and composition, trade union negotiating teams have traditionally had a 'core' team consisting of a leader, note-taker and summariser. Although this has been the traditional position, contemporary collective bargaining agendas have become increasingly more complex. This can require a team leader to include representation on the 'core' team from a special interest group or someone with a specialised knowledge, such as equal rights, health and safety, pensions, or production systems, for example. Increasingly, management are including such specialists in their negotiating team. A modern 'core' team may, therefore, comprise: leader, observer, note-taker, specialist observer/adviser(s), and summariser.

Some unions have experimented with gender-pairing of the lead negotiator's role with the objectives of extending negotiating experience to more women members and establishing a more evident women's influence on agendas and outcomes.

Ground Rules for Negotiating Team: the Preparatory Stage

Understanding the Process

Essential to the efficient performance of any negotiating team is a clear understanding of how the process they are involved in will actually work: that is, who they will be meeting, what are the procedural arrangements, including the previous and next stages, what powers the other side have to settle, what are the team's negotiating objectives and priorities.

What Job?

Each member should understand what job they are being asked to do. The note-taker should know that they are free to take notes without over-concerning themselves about their relevance or potential use. They should also know they are there to observe changes of mood, body language, etc. The summariser should be thinking about an overview of how things are progressing, what arguments made an impression, what did not. They should consider how the meeting went and what position the union is now in. If there is to be an interchange of roles during the negotiating, it is essential that everyone understands this and is given sufficient notice and preparation time.

For example, the lead negotiator may wish the observer/specialist to lead-in on a particular item, or may wish them to make a supportive statement on an item. They should understand what is expected of them and be given sufficient notice.

Who Speaks?

There should be clear agreement about who speaks and when, at the negotiating table. Apart from in certain circumstances noted above, it is common practice for lead negotiators to insist that no-one else contributes unless and until invited to do so by them. As a firm rule, it is bad practice to cut across the lead negotiator. You may inadvertently undermine your own case or bolster the other side. If someone feels strongly enough about something during the negotiations, they should indicate to the lead negotiator that they would like to come in by raising their hand, or by passing a note to the lead negotiator, or they may ask for an adjournment in the same way.

Lead negotiators should insist on having the authority to agree or refuse any such requests. However, they should be sensitive to any consensus view among the team that an adjournment is felt necessary. Equally, there is no point in slackening any pressure built up in negotiations in order to have an adjournment over something which has simply irritated a member of the team and could be left and dealt with later.

Team Decision Making

Across-the-table negotiations may take only an hour or may be spread over several hours, or days, or months, depending on the complexity or intractability of the issue(s) under negotiation. Negotiating teams, therefore, need agreement between them about how decisions are made in the interim. For example, on tactics, evaluating progress, or to discuss when and what to report back.

In a case involving a large British company the union side was faced with a difficult problem. The union had pressurised the employer over a two-year period to produce a more rational and simple wages structure covering 5,000 manual workers. The employer eventually responded in a high-profile set of negotiations, with a proposal they argued was more rational and contained less distortions than the old structure. Unfortunately for the union, the employer's first offer contained wage reductions for 1,700 union members.

To report back such a proposal could find the union being blamed for the outcome. Not to report back would be seen as a breach of privilege and rumour would persist. After lengthy and apprehensive discussion, the union negotiating team decided by majority decision to give a frank report emphasising the positive aspects of the employer's proposals and the unacceptability of the rest. Their report was endorsed but resulted in increased pressure on management to improve their offer.

In general terms informal rules should be laid down about:

- deciding tactics and strategy
- deciding adjournments
- deciding timings of meetings
- deciding about reporting back to a wider committee or members when there is
     an offer on the table
     an impasse
     a need to keep people informed about interim stages of negotiation
     new issues introduced by the employer
- checking and evaluating progress in the negotiation.

The role of the lead negotiator within the core team and in reporting back to a wider committee or members is discussed more fully in Chapter 3. Lead negotiators can decide to be active or passive in shaping attitudes at this stage towards any employer's offer or in moving or not moving towards agreement on the issue under negotiation.

Strong personal pressures on lead negotiators generally compel them to actively evaluate what is on offer and in so doing evaluate the scope for consensus or to shape attitudes around the need for greater pressure and the potential for union/employer conflict if negotiated progress remains deadlocked.

Although there is an observer/note-taker and a summariser in the core team during negotiations, it generally falls to the lead negotiator to establish consensus on what was said and precisely what was offered, if need be by checking, repeating and seeking confirmation from the other side. Inexperience can sometimes lead negotiators to miss this step, feeling that by inviting the employer to repeat and confirm an offer will allow it to slip away. Do not fall into this trap: if they refuse to confirm, you never had it anyway!

CONDITIONS FOR CONDUCTING NEGOTIATIONS

Certain basic ground rules are necessary in order to ensure that negotiations are seen to be fair and efficient:

1. the union is given equal status with management at the negotiating meeting (this means equal rights of representation to the union side with no disadvantages);
2. the place and time of the meetings are mutually agreeable;
3. the frequency of meetings suit the purposes of both parties;
4. the length of meetings is known beforehand and is mutually acceptable;
5. there are facilities for the union side to meet separately;
6. the size and composition of negotiating teams are known and acceptable.

SUMMARY

The planning stage of a particular set of negotiations can at a simple level be no more than a few hours; for other more complex or intractable issues it can take much longer. It is vital, either way, that both sides know clearly what is to be negotiated and that the union recognises it is in a negotiation position. There is little point in going to a meeting armed with facts and figures and a well-thought-out case if, when you get there, your opponent refuses to accept that the item is a legitimate item for negotiation at this stage.

Having a good negotiating team around you can be helpful in negotiations. They can, at times, help you to make more detailed and incisive responses to your opponent by drawing on their direct experiences. But careful selection, briefing and tactical use of the team is essential. The two case studies below illustrate the dangers of paying insufficient attention to selecting and briefing your team.

The conditions and arrangements for negotiations are normally not a great problem but it is best that they are mutually acceptable. There are times, however, when strained relations between the two sides can impact on these arrangements and more care has to be taken.

Case Study: Lacking Legitimacy

The management of a major charity organisation were preparing to conduct annual wage negotiations with the union representing their employees. Economic recession had brought greater demands for the charity's services. In addition, the charity business had become very competitive with each charity devising ingenious schemes in the fight to maintain their organisations and services.

Usually the annual wage negotiations were handled by a professional union officer. The charity's management had decided to 'put their cards on the table' and explain to the union the full extent of their financial plight. However, on the day, the union sent along a lay official, a branch secretary, who in fact worked for another charity organisation. The negotiations were immediately suspended with the charity management claiming that the union negotiator lacked legitimacy. They were not prepared to brief an employee of a 'competing' charity on their financial position.

Union authorisation will not suffice. Without mutually accepted legitimacy it will be rejected.

Case Study: Fiddlers Intervention

During the 1970s a statutory incomes policy was introduced by Prime Minister Ted Heath's government. The incomes policy permitted weekly increases of £1 plus 4 per cent. The 4 per cent element was deemed by the Treasury to permit 4 per cent on the 'wage bill'!

Union negotiators had rarely ever negotiated on a percentage of the wage bill so everyone got down to the task of working out what represented the 'wage bill'. Did it include bonuses, travel allowances, canteen subsidies, and other payments?

One group of workers from the Wallcovers Union despatched their negotiator off with his back-up team to squeeze the maximum out of the 4 per cent. Across the table great argument ensued over whether overtime pay could be included to calculate the magic 4 per cent figure. During several hours of argument, the lead negotiator could feel one of his shop stewards becoming increasingly impatient but who had been instructed to say nothing. Finally, when everyone was tired and tetchy, the company, with extreme reluctance, conceded that overtime pay would be taken into account in calculation of the 4 per cent. On hearing this, the impatient shop steward could contain himself no longer and exploded saying 'and I should bloody well think so, since most of the overtime in this place is fiddled in any case'. The management quickly requested an adjournment!

6

Preparing for Negotiations

In this stage we move to the detailed preparation of the case, objectives and justifying arguments. This is a key stage of the negotiations for the lead negotiator. In order to assist in understanding the process of setting objectives, and the practice of setting 'ideal' to 'fall-back' position, I have included a matrix developed by Professor John Gennard of Strathclyde University.

'Failing to prepare is preparing to fail' is a maxim negotiators ignore to their cost. A good and worthy case can be lost through a failure to properly prepare or through inept and ill-thought-out presentation. It is not simply a lack of persuasive information and argument which can cause such failures. Poor preparation and presentation can give your opponent the impression that there is a lack of conviction and union commitment to the case. Under such circumstances there is no earthly reason why you should expect the other side to concede anything. The other side of the coin is, of course, if you don't prepare, you can bet your boots the other side will. In fact, the more likely it is that you don't, the more likely your opponent will. Why shouldn't they, it makes their job all that easier.

There can, of course, be reasons for lack of preparation. Work pressures and shortage of time are the most common. The best rule for union negotiators is, if you can't prepare, don't negotiate. Alternatives might be to postpone meetings, delegate some of the preparation work, or limit the agenda of the initial negotiating meeting to an exploratory phase. Turning up for negotiations with the quite common approach of 'let's go in and hear what they have to say' puts the union in a negative position and should be avoided. Turning up with a lack of facts and information can quickly descend into no more than a point-scoring exercise. Your opponent will spot this and may insist on an immediate settlement on his/her terms.

There is, therefore, no dependable substitute for preparation. Apart from enhancing your chances of making progress, how else can you monitor success if not against parameters you set before the process began.

One further general point about preparing for negotiations: preparation cannot be viewed simply as a pre-negotiation stage, it must be seen as a continuous activity. When your arguments and facts have been tested across the table you may need to review and re-assess them, or look for new ones. If your power position suddenly changes, preparation and re-assessment may be vital.

THE COMPONENTS OF PREPARATION

There are seven components of preparation:

1. deciding whether the negotiations are likely to be adversarial or integrative in form, or whether they concern an individual grievance;
2. selecting and briefing the negotiating team;
3. researching and collating relevant information;
4. anticipating the other side;
5. assessing power positions;
6. assessing equality implications;
7. setting objectives.

Adversarial Negotiations, Integrative Negotiations or Grievance Handling?

Answering this question will, to a degree, shape the form and content of your preparation. Since sanctions are less likely in integrative negotiations, power and strategy play a less important part. The facts and information you present may necessarily be less tactical and combative. Negotiations can in these circumstances be more open and place greater emphasis on mutual gain. On issues of an economic nature the parties may be more inclined to discuss how to increase the size of the cake as well as the share. Some people regard this type of negotiation as one of style. This is in my view misleading. Union negotiators who adopt this approach as a personal 'style' without recognising the need for management reciprocity may find their openness exploited. Integrative negotiations have to be transparently a two-way process of trust and openness, though not necessarily or exclusively initiated by management.

Adversarial negotiations are not in themselves the exact converse of integrative negotiations, and some negotiations float between the two forms. However, greater attention has to be given to obtaining harder and more comprehensive facts and information, and more thought given to power and strategy in adversarial negotiations.

In Chapter 2 we discussed underlying attitudes of management negotiators. You should be anticipating that while deciding on your approach. If you decide that hostility and a non-cooperative attitude is what faces you, you must decide how to deal with it while keeping your objectives firmly in mind. It may require you to identify common interests and persuasively argue the value of joint agreement. On the other hand, if you feel you have more power at your elbow and the level of determination of your members is high, you may have to allude to that by explaining, perhaps even apologetically, the pressure you are under.

The question of which form to adopt may rest on the substance of the claim and certainly on the relationship of the parties. If an integrative approach is open to you, it is a wise move not to let a short-term dominant power position persuade you otherwise.

Individual grievance handling may involve adversarial or integrative approaches. Even on conduct problems there can be a wide difference between management and union on what is acceptable conduct or mitigation. It is not unheard of for harsh and exacting disciplinary measures to lead to a strike being provoked during a period of lean production needs, thereby saving on lay-off pay. But in general terms the one-to-one nature of individual grievances allows greater qualitative scope to pre-counsel, problem solve and shape the intended negotiated outcome.

Selecting and Briefing the Negotiation Team

Selecting and briefing for negotiations is in general terms substantially dealt with in Chapter 5. However, in specific cases the team should know the type of negotiating approach being adopted, the information to be presented and why, the objectives and strengths and weaknesses.

Researching and Collating Information

In trade union negotiations, like others, the overall objective is to reach an agreement. But there can be a wide variety of outcomes which may constitute final agreement, so as a negotiator you need information which is comprehensive, which goes beyond the specifics of the issue in hand and permits flexible responses. Professional union researchers are often asked to provide information to support demands which have been pre-set at some democratic level within the union and which permits little, if any, initial flexibility. Conversely, union negotiators handling personal cases have the opportunity to counsel members and help shape their objective.

Information, therefore, is needed firstly to decide on your objective and secondly to service that objective by its justification. Information is power, therefore it is not neutral. Some negotiators have problems with this as it can mean presenting or withholding selected information, shielding or masking events or issues. In court, for example, 'previous offences' cannot be revealed until after the court verdict and are sometimes only relevant in sentencing if they are relevant previous offences! If you have problems with this aspect of negotiations, get used to it, or get out! Of course selection, withholding or shielding must not be done crudely or naively. The case you present must be credible. If the foreman's got a black eye, he must have got it from somewhere.

In general terms, union claims are based on parity, comparability, ability to pay, self-financing share of savings, or fair, or equal treatment. On the negative side, an eye has to be kept open for consequential claims or actions.

Researching and case building can bring together a collection of facts, opinions and assumptions. Facts should be checked to see that they are facts. Opinions should be tested for strength, validity, and width of support. Counter-intuitive pieces of information can often be checked before negotiation by a non-committal enquiry to your own, or the other side. For example, 'I wonder if I can clarify something with you?' or 'try and make sense of something'. Assumptions, usually about management's intentions and attitudes, can, on rare occasions, be tested informally but more usually have to wait until the formal across-the-table negotiations. The difference between informal and formal testing of assumptions is that informal is usually on a 'private' one-to-one basis. If it reinforces beliefs and assumptions, fine – it will be believed. If it raises doubts and questions it is likely to be challenged. So 'public' testing across-the-table may be your best option.

The purpose of assembling information, particularly in personal cases, is to bring to the table new information, correct false impressions, bring a new slant, set matters in a wider context, present a legal challenge, enter mitigating factors, seek clemency, and so on. You are not asking the other side to reverse their decision or swallow their words. You are looking for a new decision in the light of the information you have brought to the negotiations and the representations you have made.

Anticipating the Other Side

This can be the most difficult part of preparations, but it must be done. It is not enough to develop your side of things; you must attempt to anticipate your opponent and develop a potential counter-response across as many areas as possible. Counter-responses are the second line in breaking down your opponent, achieving movement, gaining agreement. This involves thinking through the 'why' as well as the 'what' of your opponent's actions. Sometimes there can be a 'silent partner' in the negotiations. Your opponent may agree the equity of your case but be blocked by having other players on their side to satisfy. Part of your job is to help them out of their difficulty, to offer a route to settlement. It means the negotiations are still bilateral but now have a multilateral element which needs satisfying.

Perhaps the most public display of this feature was the 'silent' partner role played by the Conservative government in the 1984/85 miners' strike. Less dramatically, in a discipline case it could be the obduracy of a supervisor versus senior management's willingness to accept an 'exceptional circumstances' plea. Or it could be production management's concern over output, if new shift patterns are agreed by personnel management.

So looking behind what appears an entrenched position can be essential. To unblock it may mean giving assurances, satisfying concerns, correcting assumptions, or in other ways dealing with the people or concerns constraining your opponent. You cannot simply do this intuitively, you can only do it by assembling and analysing information and deploying it in purposeful argument.

Assessing Power Positions

Power in negotiations is dealt with substantially in Chapter 4. However, it has to be looked at in each specific negotiating circumstance. The general economic power position may not be of dominant concern to either of the negotiating partners in the case in question. Both sides may agree there is a matter to be settled through negotiations, and therefore power, in terms of argument and the determination of the parties, may be the factor more to the front of everyone's minds. Assessing the power position is, therefore, a practical exercise not an academic one. It is one in which your knowledge of the partners, reviewing previous negotiations, and the current climate of industrial relations, are as important as any economic, social or other external influences.

Assessing Equality Implications

Whether dealing with personal or collective cases, there is an onus on union negotiators to assess the equality implications, firstly of the case itself being put forward, but secondly of success or failure. A simple case put forward as an individual grievance by a member may, after assessment, be judged to merit a claim of discriminatory behaviour by management. Equally, pursuance of a collective claim may, if successful, be indirectly discriminatory to another group on race or gender grounds. Union negotiators should, as a matter of standard practice, make such assessments and any *prima facie* discrimination should be measured against the appropriate Code of Practice (see Appendices). More positively, negotiators should also assess what opportunities might exist in each circumstance for promoting the cause of race and gender equality.

Setting Objectives, Reconciling Priorities

Setting objectives and reconciling priorities is another area of the negotiating process which is distinguished from commercial and other forms of negotiations. Next to the information and research element, it is the largest and most crucial of the continuous preparation stage. Union negotiators are much more constrained by the internal democratic processes of the organisations they represent. They are, at times, obliged to submit and justify demands which may contain a mix of the immediate, medium, and long-term aspirations of the bargaining group they represent. On occasions negotiators can find that time and events have overtaken the gap between claim formulation and its pursuit, making things possibly more difficult.

Equally, union negotiators can be set rigid and uncompromising objectives. For example, a worker alleged to have committed a serious misdemeanour resulting in dismissal, and who proclaims complete innocence, wants nothing less than their job back and full reinstatement of rights, privileges and status. However, justice at work is based on the 'balance of probabilities' and not 'beyond all reasonable doubt' as in courts. This strengthens the employer's hand and makes it difficult for negotiators, in extreme cases, to prove innocence. In some cases it may come down to a 'plea bargain' on the 'offence' and 'sentence'.

A second example may be when governments have set down maximum wage increases under rigid formulae for incomes policies. Union negotiators have historically been charged with the responsibility of then ensuring that the maximum allowable became the minimum acceptable. To do less would be seen as one section of workers sharing greater 'wage restraint' than others.

In wage bargaining, where formal constraint policies or mechanisms do not exist, there can be implied constraint, reflecting perhaps the economic environment. Claims for increases 'in line with inflation' or 'equal to the increase in average earnings' imply an attempt to protect the value or relative value of existing earnings. Such claims intend to elicit a shared response and objective on the part of the employer. They are, therefore, not commonly intended to infer a willingness to discuss 'ideal' and 'fall-back' positions, they usually signal a fairly realistic but fixed objective.

So union negotiators can be confronted by a range of conflicting circumstances and influences, some internal, others external. How then, with these in mind, do you set about deciding objectives and reconciling priorities?

PERSONAL CASES

In personal cases, union negotiators have the opportunity to meet the member at first hand. This affords you three opportunities:

- to hear and assess all of the relevant facts, opinions, assumptions and circumstances;
- to assess not only the determination of the individual member, but also that and the degree of collective support from other members;

- to counsel the member on what, in your opinion, and in their interests, is achievable.

So personal cases afford the opportunity for setting objectives and priorities, jointly with the member. A further advantage afforded in personal cases is that so-called 'fall-back' positions can be set discreetly. In large collective claims such information is less secure and discretion less possible.

COLLECTIVE ISSUES

Setting objectives and reconciling priorities where a large group of members, with perhaps different interests, are involved in a multi-item collective claim is a somewhat more complex and inexact process. Union negotiators involved in formalised multi-item claims, where the members are not close at hand for consultation, nevertheless have to square the democratic circle of democratically determined claims, setting amended objectives and priorities, and the eventual membership ratification of negotiated outcomes. If trade unionism is to mean anything, then this principle must be adhered to. Such authority as is devolved to negotiators is always subject to ratification.

Multi-item claims are the legitimate expressions of membership wishes and aspirations. Once formalised, they become mandates for union negotiators. The problem for negotiators is that while increased income, improved income security, work quality, shorter working time and so forth are legitimate pursuits, they rarely take account of the aggregate costs of implementation. Across the negotiating table, these aggregate costs are what compel union negotiators to begin to:

- assess whether argument persuasion, equity, mutual gain or the elements of power are sufficient to bring about a comprehensively successful outcome;
- assess the determination of members to pursue the claim;
- assess employers' willingness and ability to resist;
- prioritise a response, taking these into account.

If commitment to a claim is little more than token, there is little point in continually re-stating a fixed demand. Union negotiating teams normally have delegated authority. This needs to be tapped to re-set objectives which members believe in and which will receive greater support and determination. As this task is undertaken, it becomes self-evident that striking a new balance between what members are asking for and what they are determined to get, will provide the most likely combination for negotiated success.

The process of deciding objectives and priorities is not an exact science and refinements during negotiations are normally called for. However, one reasonably systematic way of approaching the problem is offered in the Negotiator's Aspirations Matrix shown in Figure 6.1. The matrix can be used in negotiating a multi-item claim, or a single item with a number of elective components, such as a childcare agreement, or a recognition agreement. The approach simply involves the union side listing their demands down the left-hand side under objectives. The example given in Figure 6.2 is of a multi-item claim being sought.

The next stage is to prioritise the items on the objectives list, and this is done by adopting the following procedure.

1. 'Ideal' Position. The first stage is for the union negotiating team to indicate what the 'ideal' outcome of the negotiations would be from their point of view, assuming the most favourable negotiating conditions. They do this by marking 'X' against all absolutely essential items.
2. 'Realistic' Position. The team now needs to consider moving away from their 'ideal' position. This can be done on the matrix by marking with an 'X' under 'Realistic' the items you are still fully committed to achieving and with an 'O' those items you would be willing to move on. This exercise in moving to a 'Realistic' position can be done using hypothetical information for the purpose of an exercise, or using factual information in a real-life negotiating situation.
3. 'Fall-back' Position. A similar process can be carried out to establish a 'fall-back' position. As can be seen from the completed matrix in figure 6.2, the union side have used

Figure 6.1: Negotiator's Aspirations Matrix: Template

	Union/employees' three possible positions			Employers' three possible positions		
	Ideal position	Realistic position	Fall-back position	Fall-back position	Realistic position	Ideal position
Original negotiating objective						Original negotiating objective

Figure 6.2: Negotiator's Aspirations Matrix: Example 1

Original negotiating objective	Union/employees' three possible positions			Employers' three possible positions			
	Ideal position	Realistic position	Fall-back position	Fall-back position	Realistic position	Ideal position	Original negotiating objective
£10 per week increase	X	X	X	X	X	O	No increase
2 extra holidays	X	X	X	X	X	O	No extra holiday
35 hour week	X	O	O	O	O	O	No hours reduction
Improved sick pay	X	X	X	X	O	O	No improved sick pay
Childcare agreement	X	X	O	O	O	O	No childcare

75

'X' to signify the items they hope to achieve agreement on in their 'fall-back' position (that is the minimum necessary to achieve agreement) and with an 'O' those they are willing to drop or concede.

ANTICIPATING THE OTHER SIDE

In anticipating the likely response from management, the union negotiating team are asked to go back through the process a second time, only this time marking down management's response under 'ideal' conditions to them, then 'realistic', and then 'fall-back'. The negotiating teams during this exercise are asked to assume contra-pressures on management to that faced by the union at each of the stages (see Figure 6.2 right-hand columns).

As can be seen from Figure 6.2, the employer's response has been signified by placing an 'O' under the 'ideal' position, indicating that their 'ideal' position would be to concede nothing at all on any of the elements of the claim. Under the 'realistic' right-hand middle column it can be assumed that in response to argument the employer's position has changed and an 'X' has been used to signify those items on which the employer's side is willing to move. The employer's final offer under their fall-back position is marked with an 'X' on those items they are willing to move or agree on and with an 'O' on those they are sticking on. In this instance both sides appear to have secured agreement across three of the five elements of the claim. Both sides have to consider whether enough is on the table to obtain membership agreement and ratification.

The Aspirations Matrix is a valuable tool, not just at the preliminary preparation stage, but at each stage of negotiations where re-assessment and taking stock is required. It also helps to provide a disciplined approach to establishing priorities, anticipating the other side's likely responses and judging whether, at the end, a recommendable agreement is possible. Any matrix which is produced prior to the real negotiations commencing represents no more than a theoretical assessment. As across-the-table negotiations get underway, changes and refinements can be made. For example, a toned-down wage demand can be signalled in exchange for movement on childcare. Extra holidays can be actively postponed if sick pay improvements are effected immediately.

COMPETING PRIORITIES AND EQUALITY ISSUES

To repeat a point I made previously, it is at this point in negotiations that equality issues are often not prioritised. It will be observed from the matrix that there is a natural and firm 'constituency' for all of the items in the claim except childcare. Everyone will gain from extra pay, holidays, shorter hours, improved sick pay, but the constituency for childcare benefits is amorphous and 'determination power' is weakened unless attitudes have previously been shaped and continually buttressed. Not every worker, even in high female employing workplaces, anticipates having childcare responsibilities. (The assumption that men also have childcare responsibilities is recognised.) This problem must, therefore, be dealt with much earlier, essentially at claims determination stage. Solidarity support must be gained from unaffected groups. In this way you formulate a sound and durable strategy. Remember, clever tactics do not make up for a poor strategy.

CHILDCARE MATRIX

A further example in using the matrix to decide objectives and priorities is in a single-item claim, as opposed to a multi-item one. A good example of this is that of a childcare agreement which normally is made up of a number of elements each contributing to its aggregate cost. In this respect, it is similar to a multi-item claim – the elements tend to be competitive. The negotiator's job is to sort out the priorities and objectives in favour of obtaining the best achievable agreement.

Using the matrix, a claim for a childcare agreement covering a multi-worksite employer might look like Figure 6.3. The list on the left-hand column could represent the union's claim. Not surprisingly, each element making up the childcare agreement is marked with an 'X', signifying this is the union's ideal

Figure 6.3: Negotiator's Aspirations Matrix: Example 2

Original negotiating objective	Union/employees' three possible positions			Employers' three possible positions			
	Ideal position	Realistic position	Fall-back position	Fall-back position	Realistic position	Ideal position	Original negotiating objective
Workplace nursery provision	X					O	No nursey provision
75/25 pricing in employees favour	X					X	Vouchers to cover 35% of agreed costs
Pricing consistent for 1 or more children	X					X	1 child only cover
Childcare allowances to cover external childcare	X					O	NIL
Childcare allowances at nursery equivalent level	X					X	Vouchers only
Childcare vouchers equivalent level	X					X	Childcare vouchers
Admissions policy: first come first served	X					O	Priority to be given to hard to fill grades and senior staff or Personnel Dept. discretion
Union representation on users committee	X					O	N/A
Nursery wages and conditions – national agreement equivalent	X					O	N/A

position. The second task of the negotiator using the matrix is to consider the employer's likely response, bearing in mind the 'power and argument' factors weighing in the union and employer's favour. The employer's theoretical response is listed in Figure 6.3 down the right-hand column. This is marked with an 'X' on those items they are willing to move on and with an 'O' on those they are sticking on.

A union negotiator and his or her team would immediately recognise from the kind of response listed in the right-hand column of Figure 6.3 that the employer's side is hardly committed to a childcare agreement at all, and is displaying an arms-length policy by proposing to simply issue vouchers, leaving the employee to seek their own childcare arrangements. In such a position, the union would have to marshal its arguments in favour of the principles of workplace nursery provision, encouraging an improved response to voucher provision while arguing it is intended to be supplementary to workplace nursery provision and not completely substitutional. However, the union may have to consider 'bridging the gap' by indicating a willingness to move on certain elements of the claim. Tactically the union at this stage might leave to one side 'nursery conditions and terms of employment'. Such items may raise 'thorny' institutional issues at the wrong time. For example, the employer may wish to retain the option of contracting out the staffing and running of the nursery even though it is a workplace provision. Allowing the union at the workplace negotiating rights for the nurseries may lead to higher pay rates than can be obtained otherwise and also close down the option to contract out nursery services.

The union's new 'realistic' position is listed in the left-hand column of Figure 6.4. The union have now conceded that vouchers instead of cash allowances are acceptable and reduced the number of elements of the claims from nine to eight. the items they are still committed to are marked with an 'X'. The employer's 'realistic' position is listed in the right-hand middle column, indicating that they are willing to move to a limited provision of workplace nurseries and move on nursery pricing policy, but still wish to retain a voucher element, and are still some distance from the union side on admissions policy and management of the nurseries. This position is marked with an

Figure 6.4: Negotiator's Aspirations Matrix: Example 3

Original negotiating objective	Union/employees' three possible positions				Employers' three possible positions		Original negotiating objective
	Ideal position	Realistic position	Fall-back position	Fall-back position	Realistic position	Ideal position	
Workplace nursery provision		X			X		No nursery provision key/major sites
2/3 employer 1/3 employee pricing		X			X		1/3 employer 2/3 employee pricing
Pricing consistent for 1 or more children		X			X		2 children matrix
Childcare allowances at nursery equivalent level		X			O		NIL
Childcare vouchers at 2/3 nursery equivalent		X			X		Childcare vouchers equal to 1/3 nursery price
Admissions policy to favour low paid and second child		X			O		Admissions policy to reflect management and union priorities
Union representation on users' committee		X			O		Parents nominate users' committee
Nursery staff wages to be negotiated at local level		X			O		Nursery staff wages to reflect market

80

'X' for those items they are willing to move on and an 'O' for those they are still sticking on.

The union negotiator in this position is now faced with a clear tactical dilemma. Pressing for workplace nursery provision at an increased number of sites may throw up aggregate costs disproportionately and the unavailability of suitable premises may delay the practical implementation of the agreement. On the other hand, vouchers will become a substitution for many members but jacking up the 'voucher subsidy' could mitigate against more nursery places at each site.

Management, for their part, are extremely reluctant to get too involved in the childcare business which workplace nurseries draw them towards. On the other hand, having got round to discussing it seriously with the unions, they can now see the positive side of a flexible childcare agreement and are willing to move forward cautiously on the level of assistance to be offered.

Union and management now need to move towards their fall-back position which is listed in Figure 6.5. It can be seen from this theoretical exposition that both sides have moved closer together. The union have conceded that workplace nurseries will be limited to major sites but with a 12-month review. Management agree with this. On pricing policy the union has moved to a price banding policy but with protection for the lower paid. Management have done likewise but there is still a gap on how much they are willing to pay. Both sides have agreed that vouchers have to be at levels equivalent to the bandings. On admissions policy the union has conceded that the policy needs to reflect employer and employee priorities but there is still a gap. On the users' committee the employer is still committed to excluding the union, and on nursery staff wages and conditions is making no commitment.

The union have, under the left-hand fall-back column, marked with an 'X' those items they are still committed to. The employer's side, in the right-hand fall-back column, have marked with an 'X' those items where in their view they have now moved sufficiently to have obtained agreement. They have also marked with an 'O' those items which they are sticking to and are unwilling to concede any further. By dropping their claim for cash allowances in favour of vouchers and by

Figure 6.5: Negotiator's Aspirations Matrix: Example 4

Original negotiating objective	Union/employees' three possible positions			Employers' three possible positions			Original negotiating objective
	Ideal position	Realistic position	Fall-back position	Fall-back position	Realistic position	Ideal position	
Workplace nursery provision in all major sites with 12 month review			X	X			Workplace nurseries in all major sites with 12 month review
Banded pricing policy with 2/3 minimum subsidy for lower paid			X	O			Banded pricing policy with 50% subsidy to low paid and second child
Childcare vouchers based on nursery banding level			X	X			Childcare vouchers based on nursery banding levels
Admissions policy to prioritise management and employee needs with annual review			X	X			Admissions policy to permit priority to staff shortages and low paid
One parent one union nominee on users committee			X	O			One parent nominee on management committee
Nursery staff wages sufficient to attract qualified staff			X	O			Nursery staff wages to reflect market

agreeing to the principle of a banding pricing policy, the union side have reduced the elements of the original claim from nine to six and have agreement over three, with one other (banding levels) close to agreement.

The management side would in this circumstance have to consider whether they had offered enough to secure agreement. A misjudgement about this could be costly as is explained earlier in this text. For the union, a judgement has to be made. Is this the best achievable result in the circumstances? Are sanctions justifiable and a realistic prospect, or has agreement now been reached?

SUMMARY

Preparation is all. Without it, your opponent will recognise your weakness. Having said that, preparation is, of course, also a discipline. Gathering facts and information, working out objectives and priorities, deciding strategy, tactics and approach, anticipating your opponent's response, all take time.

The route to make that easier is to have a simple checklist you can use on each occasion:

- who am I meeting and what should be my approach?
- what facts and information do I need?
- what are the issues?
- what are my objectives – what do I hope to come out with?
- what is my opponent's response likely to be?
- what are my strategy and tactics?
- what are my options if agreement cannot be reached?

The Aspirations Matrix can also be utilised, as you will have seen, as a form of additional checklist in setting down the issues and deciding objectives and priorities.

7

Across-the-Table Negotiations

What has been discussed so far in this text has been the background and preparation work for negotiations. We now move to the step where that preparatory work is tested out in the face-to-face meeting with your negotiating opponent. This chapter draws together the wide range of matters which have to be dealt with at this stage:

1. setting the tone and climate;
2. case presentation;
3. receiving the other side's response;
4. the argument stage;
5. extracting an offer.

In addition to managing the negotiations as they pass through these five phases, negotiators must be listening to and observing what is happening across the table; dealing with deadlines and adjournments; deciding and monitoring tactics and the whole general conduct and progress of the negotiations. We will look at these issues later in the chapter. The closing of negotiations will then be discussed in Chapter 8.

SETTING THE TONE AND CLIMATE

Most negotiating sessions at work are conducted between people who are familiar or known to each other. Both sides may reach a stage where they know each other's strengths, weaknesses and style. Tone and climate-setting in such situations can simply be a ritual courtesy based on the personal disposition of the parties. Such ritual courtesies do, of course, have their place; without them motives and intentions can be misread. However, skills in setting the desired climate for negotiation reach beyond the ritualistic practice. They should equip the negotiator not only to recognise if the desired climate has been set, but to consciously monitor during negotiations whether it has been maintained, improved or deteriorated. That can mean looking behind the veneer of pleasantries and judging whether the mood is changing and why.

The very opening stages of across-the-table negotiations are the most vital in climate-setting. Frequently, the climate has been greatly influenced by what has happened before the meeting. Inexperienced negotiators often feel that they must automatically reflect the emotions of anger, indignation or frustration of those they represent. This is not so. Playing to the gallery is an easily detected tactic which, once recognised, weakens your own position and confuses your opponent about your real feelings on the matter and what can safely be offered.

Another equally common fallacy is to believe it is too difficult to alter a climate already created by others before the negotiations commence. Positive initiatives at the opening of negotiations have a greater and more lasting impression than what has gone before. In fact, skilful handling can neutralise a damaging and inhibiting prelude. It should be remembered that the reverse is also the case and that damaging opening remarks can wipe out a helpful climate carefully cultivated at a preliminary stage.

The key aim for negotiators in the opening moments of negotiation is to ensure that what they say and do contributes to establishing a durable rapport with the other side. Once practised in different negotiating situations it becomes part of the negotiator's package of skills. It is to these practical and common sense steps that we now turn.

Climate creation in negotiations is the lubricant of the negotiating process. For trade union negotiators that lubricant is there to serve three purposes: to ensure the consensus to negotiate is maintained, to assist the process of obtaining a first offer, and to reach agreement. The first and most obvious thing is that to serve all three purposes 'climate conditions' have to be durable. To achieve this you have to look behind the opening moments of negotiation to see what is in the mind of the other partner to the negotiation.

There are few occasions when management negotiators will come to the table bristling with confidence about the task in front of them. Doubts, uncertainty, and a defensive posture frequently cloud the thoughts of management negotiators before entering the room. In that sometimes taut frame of mind, it can be difficult for a union negotiator to get fluidity into the process. You should, therefore, be conscious of the fact that initial verbal contact on neutral/non-business matters, such as personal interests, will be more reassuring and relaxing than immediately confronting your opponent on the issues of the day in a strident tone. This stage also provides a last minute opportunity to obtain information or re-check facts or timings. In Britain these meeting courtesies are usually informal, almost casual. In other countries they are conducted with varying degrees of formality and politeness – a matter to be seriously considered as transnational bargaining and new consultative structures emerge.

The second feature of these initial contacts is that of establishing a feeling of trust and integrity between you and your negotiating adversary. This needs to be done at two levels: first, between the two parties as negotiators; and second, as negotiators dealing with the particular issues under negotiation. Trust and integrity in this form can only be established over the longer term. However, it is possible at a single meeting to establish a sufficiently genuine degree by such matters as:

- the degree of openness in your approach;
- expressing empathy with a known problem of the other's side;
- referring to past dealings with people known to the other side.

The final part of the climate creation phase is 'getting down to business'. This should result from a friendly but formal break from the preliminary phase. This may be done by moving into another room or taking your place at a negotiating table, or if already seated, opening your notes and signalling your intention to begin. Negotiations are usually held in premises where management have control over the physical environment but there is no reason why the break to 'get down to business' should not be called by the union. Indeed there can be some minor advantage: it establishes a degree of control over that part of the meeting and permits the union to influence the opening pace of the negotiation.

Each negotiator, male and female, has their own personal style and approach to these things and the objectives are the same for both. What you do, how you do it, and how you respond is a matter for you and how it serves its purpose.

CASE PRESENTATION

When the formal negotiations begin it is usually up to those making the claim to start by presenting their case. Case presentation is done in three parts: stating your grievance or demand; putting forward the argument and justification to support it; and summarising your proposition.

Stating Your Grievance or Demand

In some circumstances your case may have been submitted in writing beforehand, in which case you should have re-read the written submission and taken a copy with you in case you are asked questions on it or any parts require clarification, or, as can happen, basic facts of the case are in dispute.

However, you are not there to read through your written submission, no matter how clever or vital you feel it to be. Remember what has been said about attention spans. You are only going to have the other side's undivided attention for a few short minutes. You need, therefore, some written notes of the case. Even where the case is a simple one and no written submission was made or was necessary, no competent negotiator should start without the basic facts and key points written down in note form. Referring to your notes, you should state your claim or grievance briefly. In a substantive claim it is generally a good idea at an early point to list, with whatever emphasis is justified, the things you are looking for agreement on.

In essence, make it clear at the outset what you want. If there are some 'old chestnuts' in your claim which are now priority items, state that at the earliest point in the opening statement. That means you may have laid emphasis on some element of your claim in the past, but you now have to distinguish between people's attitudes then and now by highlighting this in your opening presentation. In that way you afford management the opportunity to take account of this when responding to your claim. If their response is still negative to that element of your claim, you equally have a more informed opportunity to assess the necessary strength of your counter-response.

It is at this stage that equality issues stay firmly in place or start to slide. The union's priorities and attitudes need to be struck publicly across the table. Shaping attitudes on new agenda issues at this stage is vital. Equally, union negotiators will be conscious of management's awareness of the disaggregated and often amorphous constituency of some equality demands, making unity and militancy difficult to achieve.

In the case of individual grievances, it is important that you not only state the grievance but propose a solution. Management will not thank you for an approach which states your member's grievance but leaves them with the residual problem of working out what to do. Often this is simple and straightforward: 'We think Mrs Thomson's written warning for unsatisfactory work should be removed. Our own enquiries reveal that she was on maternity leave when training on the new procedures took place. We suggest that she receive training at the earliest possible time and, in the meantime, be given special support from her supervisor.' In other cases things are not as straightforward and 'creative' remedies are required.

Case Study: Creative Tailors

The pace of work and output of cutters in clothing and tailoring factories in the North East of England was controlled by the

Tailors Log. The Log listed the time to be taken for each cloth-cutting operation and thereby the output for the day and week. The Log was recognised by both the tailors' union and employers as ostensibly representing a fair day's work. However, many cutters using their own refinements to cutting methods could finish work hours ahead of normal stopping time, or even be days in front with completed work secretly stockpiled. This led to workplaces being invaded with gambling, hobbies and pastimes of cutters trying to secretly while away their spare time at work. The employers pressed and argued for the Log to be scrapped and higher output to be attained because customer demand was so great.

The problem was, most cutters were already working regular mid-week and weekend overtime. In addition, a sizeable minority of cutters could barely achieve the existing Log output levels. Revising them would lead to unreasonable pressure on some cutters. More importantly, according to the Log, if cutters did do more work than the Log required in a day or week they could not be paid any more for doing so. If they revised the Log, other cutters would feel threatened. The problem seemed to be without solution.

Some genius came up with the solution. Why not invent another 'day' and compress it into each week. 'Let's call it the "compression day". The existing Log would apply to the "compression day" but each worker could individually decide whether to "work" the imaginery day or not.' Everyone went home happy. A win–win solution.

Case Study: Size is Not Everything

A middle-ranking civil servant found that his new office relocation was not satisfactory. He was, in accordance with his grade and rank, entitled to an office of a certain size befitting that rank. He found, after careful measurement, his office was two feet shorter and eighteen inches narrower than he was entitled to. He complained to his union who could not deny he had a genuine grievance but, short of knocking the whole office block down and rebuilding, there did not seem to be a solution, as all other offices for his rank had been allocated.

His union officer came up with the 'creative remedy'. Civil servants one rank above were given desks with leather inlays and two ranks above were given larger desks. He was allocated a larger desk including leather inlay and was as happy as a fox among chickens.

Your Argument and Justification

Having presented your demands, you now have to put forward the reasoning, facts and arguments to justify and support your demands. You should do this briefly, selecting only your strongest points at this stage; weaker ones will tend to dilute your case and perhaps be pounced on by the other side. There are three other reasons why you should not present all your arguments immediately. First, you are not there to empty your head; by that time your audience will have lost interest at best or become irritated and reactionary at worst. Second, your objective at this stage is to create interaction. This is best achieved by being brief and simple, not long-winded and complex. Complexities are best dealt with at a later stage by being peeled back in layers, not rushed at in complex monologues.

Lastly, if there are any special or obvious weaknesses in your case, the justification stage of the negotiation may be the opportune time to deal with them. This is not a rule, it is a judgement. If you set them out in context and mitigate them successfully, you can defuse or blunt management's exposure of them. You may even enhance your case by making it clear you have thought the matter through clearly and even-handedly. If you feel it appropriate, you can turbo-charge this by offering the union's support to prevent recurrence.

On the other hand, you may feel it better to gain some ground first and deal with weaknesses as they arise. If you decide that 'wait and see' is your tactical preference, you should have assessed how your weakness will strengthen the other side and how much damaged will be done to your position if your weakness is exposed. As said, it is judgement time!

If your negotiating team contains a specialist, for example on equality bargaining or health and safety, you should by now have sorted out whether and how and when you are going to use them at this stage. It is imperative that you, as lead negotiator, 'manage' this aspect of the representation. Specialists need to be guided by the same rules and constraints as you are. Their contribution should, therefore, be a cameo role, a second layer to your contribution. The management team may not contain matching specialists, therefore over-zealous or ridiculing comments should be ruled out.

Alternatively, a special observer representing a minority group may need guidance and support to get over their key points. The lead negotiator must assume that responsibility and provide a satisfactory and empathetic lead-in. Special representatives or observers provide an ideal opportunity to support general points with specific examples about how this or that is affecting a particular group or person. Management negotiators welcome this as it is something concrete they can check out and rely upon to justify their later responses. If specialists are inclined to be over-zealous or complex, then equally lay observers have a tendency to feel that exaggeration is necessary to push their point home. As lead negotiator, your responsibility is to manage this.

Summarising your Proposition

The third part of case presentation is the summary. Your summary should have four objectives. It should:

- summarise the demands you are making and the remedies you seek;
- summarise why you are making the demands, your members' feelings on the issues and your justifying arguments. You may wish to bring in your specialists and observer representatives again at this point;
- invite questions and clarification;
- build upon the co-operative and business-like climate you hopefully have already created.

If your negotiations are of the integrative type you may wish to re-emphasise what, in your view, are any points of common interest, or any gain for the employer which you may have in mind. By finalising such points, you are attempting to motivate your opponent into giving a positive response.

Following the summary of the presentation there is no set way in which negotiations proceed. You may find that after some questions and clarification there is an initial and limited response to your submission or you are simply thanked for your submission and the meeting is adjourned. However, in a less formal and structured meeting you may find that the other side, having previous knowledge of your grievance/claim and likely submission, is ready to respond immediately.

Tactical Considerations on Presentation

Consideration needs to be given by the negotiating team and particularly the lead negotiatior to the tactical approach to be used in the presentation of claim within a single negotiation, whether broken by adjournments or not. Case presentation can be of three sorts: single item, multi-item interconnected or multi-item unconnected.

Single item claims may be substantive or procedural. They may also be items that can be more easily dealt with by a more integrative problem-solving approach. If this is the case, tactical consideration needs to be given to the degree of openness that is appropriate. On the other hand, you might wish to consider when it is best to raise a matter. Timing can be a power factor in negotiations and is further dealt with in Chapter 10.

Multi-item claims are, of course, subject to the same considerations. However, additional tactical considerations are required according to whether the items are interconnected or unconnected. An example of an interconnected multi-item claim may be an annual pay and conditions claim. A multi-item unconnected claim may consist of a number of items brought together under a single set-piece negotiation with little more connection than their implementation cost.

Two parties coming together to negotiate usually have an agenda, a list of items on which they know they are expected to negotiate. However, the agenda may have been thrown together some time earlier and may or may not reflect priorities. It may, therefore, be regarded by a lead negotiator and those raising the claim as no more than a list from which a tactical approach has to be decided upon. The two most frequent approaches used are the parallel approach and the sequential approach.

The parallel approach is one in which you, as lead negotiator, try to move all items of the claim forward simultaneously. That is, at each step in the preparation stage and subsequent stages of the negotiation you attempt to give equal emphasis and weight to each item and urge concessions on each. (As concessions are made on some items you can prioritise the others to maintain the parallel pattern of negotiating pressure.) Total success using this tactical approach, like any other, is not guaranteed. However, practice will help negotiators to develop a rhythm and skill in using this approach.

Two further points on the parallel approach. First, it does attempt to deal fairly with the democratic pressures on the lead negotiator. You are not knocking items off the agenda or failing to reach them, as can happen in other approaches. Prioritisation and successful outcomes develop as a part of the negotiation and interaction process. Second, new bargaining priorities can be seen to have been pushed equally. Minority interests can be included in the general dynamic and momentum of the claim; a point sought after for a long time by those interested in equality bargaining.

The second tactical approach is the sequential approach. This approach is used in some circumstances by negotiators whether the claim contains items that are interconnected or unconnected. It basically means taking one item at a time and going into it in some depth and time, looking for concessions before moving on to the next item. Here again the agenda for the negotiation may be little more than a list which is then prioritised, usually by the side making the claim. That frequently can mean the lead negotiator seeking consensus with the other side on the sequence of items to be negotiated.

The key tactical advantage of this approach is the flexibility it allows the lead negotiator. For example, you may feel that leading with the highest cost item on the agenda serves you best. You may think that getting agreement on low-cost items first would allow the other side a tactical advantage to say 'we have agreed 75 per cent of your list – we have been as reasonable as we can'.

Alternatively, lead negotiators often feel that lists they are expected to negotiate are cluttered and cumbersome, and prefer to reduce the number of items as quickly as possible. The second strand to this tactical approach is to choose those items that are low cost to management but highly valued by your membership.

An additional advantage in taking this route is that as items are agreed, by emphasising 'progress towards full agreement' you are more likely to get the other side in an agreeing mood. A further key disadvantage to this approach is that the other side may recognise the low-cost/high-value aspect of your approach and the advantage it offers them. In that case, you may find they have privately agreed to concede at an early stage, but held back agreement on the low-cost items, and eventually package them together, conditional on your recommending a low compromise offer on the high-cost item. You can then be faced with what looks like an attractive, highly valued offer and membership pressure to agree to something which, in the long run, will look increasingly less attractive.

Case Presentation – The Contentious Agenda

Agendas are an area in which union negotiators have a particular responsibility. You have to decide whether it is appropriate to place certain items on an agenda or not. The most frequent judgement to be made is one of timing. Would it be tactically better to place an item on the agenda now or later? On other occasions it can be the form and content of the item. An item expressed with positive connotations will receive more consideration than a negative one. Some of these problems can be avoided if you can get the opportunity to consult with the other side.

The most hazardous and contentious route to take is to try to force items on to the agenda in which the other side have no firm legitimacy or constitutional authority. This problem can most easily occur where negotiating machinery has been changed or decentralised. Even more fraught with difficulty is the situation in which new union or employer confederal negotiating bodies have been formed. Too much pressure on such bodies to extend their constitutional remit can fracture relationships and the bodies may disintegrate completely. You can write rules about this but at the end of the day it has to be sorted out through intra-union and intra-organisational discussion, otherwise you may find yourself without a negotiating partner.

What Role for Management in Case Presentation?

If part of the process of case presentation for a negotiator involves anticipating the thoughts and responses of the other side, what then may management's role be in this process? Clearly, in some circumstances a management negotiator may feel they have more to gain by withholding information until the right tactical moment. On the other hand, management negotiators, by keeping silent or shielding information, may allow unrealistic expectations to build up. In a trade union setting this can lead to a union and its negotiators being locked in by a democratic decision that is being overrun by a newly emerging economic background to the negotiations. In such situations, union negotiators are frequently between a rock and a hard place. To support and explain the new economic rationale can seem like betrayal, not to do so can mean the negotiations foundering. More dangerously, confrontation may follow in an environment in which the workers' power position is much less favourable than they originally believed. Feelings among workpeople that they have been pulled on to the punch merely serve to embitter industrial relations. With the right motivations and skills, management negotiators can have a constructive influence on claims as well as settlements. However, ritualistic pleadings of poverty can lead to cynicism on the part of negotiators and those they represent.

Management responses to multi-item claims will focus on the advisability of introducing any particular proposal; the projected cost of it; the aggregate cost of all the items being claimed; and lastly, any priority being attached to an item by the other side.

When representing workers, negotiators have to plan how they are going to deal with resistance in all four areas. If the aggregate cost is the problem, as it most often is, you need to consider whether it is necessary to prioritise or even drop items in the claim to make progress with the rest. Of course, if you decide to drop certain items but don't tell the other side, they may think you are harbouring thoughts about returning to them and refuse to move. But remember, don't make heroic unilateral sacrifices. It is the 'if we were to ...', 'would you ...' approach you want!

RECEIVING MANAGEMENT'S RESPONSE

This phase of the negotiation is an important point in the whole process. It is here that both sides will find out if they are heading for agreement or possibly for the rocks, and the behaviour of both sides can be important. By this stage management may have listened to your submission in polite silence, save a few questions and points of clarification, responded to, perhaps, with equal politeness in an atmosphere of mutual trust and respect. However, your submission may have been interrupted by the odd acid remark or the occasional threat, or you may be about to find out that the other side's polite silence was just that, and is about to break into something with a rougher edge. They may be about to tell you about how much you overrate your members' work performance and underrate their many shortcomings. On the other hand, the response may be amicable and business-like.

If the negotiation is to move into a productive mode, your response must be to listen, do not interject, do not threaten and equally do not be intimidated by threats. Above all, think about how negative you feel about people who try to score points off you – so don't you do it to someone from whom you are trying to evoke a positive response. Equally, it should go without saying for union negotiating teams that sexist, racist or bigoted remarks anywhere in the negotiating situ are ruled out, otherwise you may find your meeting adjourned and diaries full for a considerable time.

So it is not simply your intellectual response but your behavioural reaction at this stage which will determine how well constructive progress will be made. The skills of negotiating are as much about controlling behavioural responses as they are about incisive intellectual argument. So let us look at two of these skills, 'listening and observing' and 'asking qeustions'.

Listening and Observing

It sounds simple but it isn't. It can be mentally and physically demanding and emotionally frustrating, but it can be the key to a successful outcome. Your opponent will, while speaking, send signals, admit errors, provide clues, reveal weaknesses and strengths. Listening in negotiation is, therefore, about more than patience and forbearance. Listening positively to what your opponent is saying can mean listening closely for clues and ideas on how to move negotiations forward. Listening hard despite distractions and a provocative delivery requires practice and skill. Primarily it is what is said you want to know, not how it is said and by whom. So, if necessary, and at the right time, you can shoot the message, but never the messenger. Provocative behaviour can be a deliberate tactic to force you to break off negotiations, sometimes for no other reason than to buy time. On the other hand, the pest who in mid-negotiations accepts all incoming phone calls has to be dealt with. If it is their office, all you can do is ask politely, even emphatically, for them to be stalled or diverted. In someone else's premises, there may be other alternatives.

Half-listening and half-formulating a counter-response with body langugage that says 'I'm bursting to come in at the first pause' sends a signal to the other negotiator that a perhaps thoughtful and well-prepared response is not respected – this can be the first stage to blocking an offer by not allowing it to open up.

So listening closely, positively and constructively does require patience, practice and skills development. Practising it in actual negotiations will lead you naturally towards 'enquiring skills', that is to ask questions of your opposite number. Doing so sends a different signal, it says 'I am listening and taking your comments seriously' – maybe it will provoke your opponent to do the same.

The constant and conscious practice of listening skills during negotiations can develop them so that you are perceptive but not impressionable; you can take cognisance of what you have heard without being overly influenced; you become sensitive to the implications of what is being said but are not bowled over; and you become discerning and discriminatory about what you hear. This is the mark of a skilful negotiator. The ability to allow counter-arguments to be taken in, set alongside existing convictions and commitments, evaluated and responded to is a skill which must be learned and practiced.

THE ARGUMENT STAGE – GETTING THINGS MOVING

Having presented, summarised and clarified your claim or grievance, and having received and listened to the other side's response, the negotiations invariably need to move from this structured and formal approach to a process that has more fluidity. It may be thought that if you and the other side are simply stating and re-stating your preferred position and both sides are doing no more than listening, albeit intently, that negotiations will simply dry up and end in the ditch. This can be avoided by moving from the more formal statement and response stage and switching to one involving asking hypothetical questions and making 'risk-free' statements.

At this stage some negotiators set themselves what may be described as process objectives. These are 'find out objectives' designed to probe the other side's position, test their commitment, their willingness to move, uncover hidden blockages to progress, assess what reciprocal responses may be necessary. Setting yourself process objectives can be undeclared but can assist you, first, to obtain movement, and second, to influence the shape of the outcome. This tactical method of obtaining movement is common to all sorts of negotiation situations and can be deployed by both union and management. The hypothetical nature of the questions or statements protect either side from being interpreted as having offered a concession.

Management may wish to use this method for a number of reasons. They may not have the authority to formally concede their 'hypothetical' proposition. They may wish to simply test the water for a particular proposal, or they may wish to add conditions before making a further formal offer. In a broad general sense, such an approach is healthy for the negotiation itself, as it indicates that management are trying to move towards agreement.

Union negotiators, on the other hand, can find this tactical method particularly useful in probing the other side and in searching for agreement. The democratic nature of a union negotiator's role can place constraints on how flexible they can be in negotiations. The use of hypothetical questioning and propositioning techniques can ease this difficulty and create movement in negotiations.

The method itself simply involves the use of the 'what if' question. 'What if ... you end-loaded the wage deal, would this help?' 'What if ... we were to consider a different implementation date?' The list of 'what if' questions is endless and their importance is twofold. First, they should be relevant and probing, and second, the answers should therefore be equally worth listening to intently. It is not relevant and indeed is damaging to start asking 'what if' questions that call for radical change to what is already on offer if you have already noticed or acknowledged that the other side were generally moving in the right direction. Damaging 'what if' questions have been exploited to adjourn negotiations and delay settlements. So the tactic has its limits – don't overdo it.

'Risk-free' or non-committal statements can generally be stated in the form 'If you were willing to ... we could take it back to the members/branch committee' or 'we could consider it'. There are many variations of the 'risk-free', 'without commitment' questions and statements, a few more examples are:

- 'how would you feel if ...'
- 'supposing you/we were to ...'
- 'have you considered ...'

These methods can be used by both union and management negotiators. If you wish to further encourage a positive response, you can add a rider that it may:

- help to close the gap;
- gain a favourable response from the members;
- move us closer to agreement.

By dealing with suggestions and proposals in this way, it gets them into the negotiating forum without formal commitment by either side. It should be borne in mind that all parties to negotiations suffer from 'quicksand phobia', a feeling that the earth will open up underneath them if they agree to something too quickly and before they feel sure-footed. Also, if firmer proposals do arise from a 'risk-free' discussion, they appear to have jointly emerged and so avoid the 'loss of face' that frequently inhibits negotiations and settlement.

Further points on this approach:

1. You should brief your negotiating team that you are going to use this method and why, otherwise they may wonder what is going on and make damaging interruptions.
2. Do not commit the members to agreeing something you have floated.
3. If management use this technique, be careful not to get bounced into agreeing something. There is no reason for it, other than inexperience. Ask for a break/adjournment to consult your committee members or make a telephone call etc. On the other hand, if you are in a position to respond – do it. If your response is positive it will encourage fluidity. If negative, it will stop management harbouring false hopes.

4. Union negotiators should avoid over-playing the 'we have no mandate or authority from the members to agree/discuss or negotiate this'. It can be used as a feint, but may be taken literally and opportunities may be lost. Equally, over-use can make union negotiators sound weak, not in command of the situation, unable to deliver final agreement, and so make concession-making more hazardous for the other side.

5. If management use this method to float 'conditional' offers, then invariably the condition will come first and the offer second. In doing so, the trick for management is to play down the conditions and play up the value of the concession. Union negotiators have to keep their eye on the ball with such offers. If necessary split the conditions and the offer and evaluate them separately. If one heavily outweighs the other, you have more negotiating to do.

EXTRACTING AN OFFER

Easing the Path for Improved Offers

Difficult as cases can sometimes be, the path to settlement can sometimes become unnecessarily blocked or impeded by the presence in the negotiations of other non-substantive barriers. Chief among these and present in all of us, are the twin tendencies which feed upon each other: the unwillingness in all of us to change our position (the 'why me' syndrome) and a tendency to gloat on others who do. The role of the trade union negotiator must extend itself by easing the path for improved offers by dealing with both these tendencies and in so doing making it easier for management to improve its offer.

This can be done in several ways.

1. By identifying and giving emphasis to the advantages to management of a more satisfactory offer or settlement. Teachers, traditionally, have emphasised the value to education of having well-paid teachers. More contemporaneously in equality bargaining, union negotiators have

pointed to the advantages of attracting and retaining trained staff who are working mothers.

2. By complementing rather than castigating improved but low offers. Union negotiators who wish to give vent to their feelings by punishing low or inadequate offers may inhibit improvements and do their members no service. A simple statement that says 'we appreciate your attempt to be helpful but ...' will gain a more positive reaction.

3. By moderating the value of an offer to the trade union side. Management may have given a lot of consideration to where to pitch their offer; exuberance from the union side, verbal or otherwise, will dent their confidence about making further gestures – particularly in a multi-item claim.

4. By steering either the union or management side away from fixed and entrenched positions that will involve a major loss of face to change. This does not mean you cannot be resolute in your demands, but the more 'public' your fixed position becomes the more loss of face involved and the higher the cost. Witness the titanic 1984/85 battle of Thatcher v. NUM and the public loss of face problem this involved. Throughout the strike Thatcher made high-profile public statements stating and re-stating her fixed position. However, the miners' leader kept doing the same thing.

For union lead negotiators these can be matters that have to be skilfully handled not only across the negotiating table but in the wider negotiating forum. This can mean reaching consensus and discipline within the negotiating team or involve intra-union bargaining referred to earlier in this text.

What is an Offer?

So what is an 'offer'? Each union–management negotiation is not an isolated and separate event. For the most part they are part of a continuum. The parties are familiar to each other. Agreements reached are often simply revisions of, or extensions to, existing agreements. In that climate, offers can more easily be made directly. In other circumstances, however, this may not be the case and union negotiators have to sharpen their instincts for identifying offers that are intentionally guarded or unconsciously signalled. Simple, even obvious you might think. Unfortunately stories abound among personnel directors of negotiators who could not read an offer unless it was explicitly made.

Here then are some examples of offers and possible union responses.

Preliminary Offer

For example, an offer in response to a union claim for an improved childcare agreement might be: 'Well we've looked at your submission and listened to what you've had to say and what we would like to propose is that we will conduct a survey/review and if your points are borne out we will certainly call another meeting and discuss them with you.'

Is this a genuine preliminary offer? Is it a stall or a time-wasting strategy? As it stands, it is an offer to conduct a survey/review. A union negotiator would want to test its intention and integrity by agreeing a timescale for its conduct, union participation in it, and a management agreement in principle to improve things if facts are borne out.

Initial/Opening Offer

For example: 'In response to the union's claim for a 10 per cent wage/salary increase in the quite desperate current trading conditions and in order to protect employment, we are willing to offer on the review date of 1 April an increase of 4 per cent on all grades with a further 1.5 per cent on 1 October. We cannot concede anything on holidays or working time.'

This offer represents less than half the union's claim of wages and no concessions in other parts of the claims. However, it is a direct offer. Managements rarely make first and final offers unless they feel they are in a dominant power position. There is therefore scope to seek an improved offer. Union negotiators should avoid 'low offer frustration' from descending into cynicism in which the offer or the messengers bringing it are subjected to ridicule. It is also the lead negotiator's job to restrain his team. You don't punish the initial offer, you encourage an improvement.

Conditional/Qualified Offer

Experience has shown that when making conditional/qualified offers, management will, as a rule, state their conditions first as a concrete demand, and the concessionary part of their offer second, and in a tentative manner. For example: 'If you will accept new flexible work arrangements and multi-machine working we will feel in a position to consider an improved financial offer.'

The reason for making conditional offers in this manner is to ensure tactical advantage to management by getting union agreement on the 'conditions' in the bag first, then bringing forward a new offer that relates to the original claim and members aspirations, rather than separately calculating the value of the 'conditions' conceded by the union.

This isn't an offer to calculate the value of future savings arising from multi-machine working and new working practices. It is an offer to consider bridging the difference between what has already been offered and what management thinks your members will accept regardless of any extra value generated by improved efficiency.

Union negotiators are at a disadvantage with such offers. First, because they are unlikely to have sufficient information to evaluate future savings, and any attempt will be time-consuming and inevitably speculative. Second, they will be under pressure to achieve a settlement equal to the members' realistic expectations.

A range of separate or complementary responses may be to:

- emphasise to members the notional value of the 'conditions' in an attempt to shape attitudes towards the value of the total package;
- press home the maximum notional value to management;

- try to establish criteria for a future review of the value of savings.

Alternatively, a non-committal questioning session might be most fruitful. For example, you could open with: 'Supposing for the sake of argument I was to go back to my committee with your proposal for work practice changes, what, from your point of view, can I tell them about the total value and distribution of the savings arising from these changes, as I am sure it would interest them.' This tactic has the effect of splitting of the 'conditions' for consideration as a separate item.

Implied Offer

Some negotiators feel that implied offers are not offers at all but simply indicators or signals from management that their reservations, opposition or intransigence is qualified. Some negotiators prefer to read such indicators or signals as offers as they imply a conditional willingness to make a formal offer. Seen in that light, union negotiators should use such offers to sharpen their negotiating instincts. Listening, reading between the lines, identifying implied offers, then fleshing them out, is a basic negotiating skill as these examples illustrate.

'We believe our holiday provision is above average for the industry and as such are not willing to improve it' – so if we can prove it is not, you will look at it again!

'We cannot afford to improve the holiday provision in the current holiday year' – so next year is a possibility!

'With our current labour-attraction problems we will be opposing any claim for an across-the-board increase' – so differential increases are on!

'Absenteeism is costing the company a fortune but childcare arrangements seem an expensive solution' – so we can talk about it!

Implied offers are, therefore, not offers to accept or reject, they are offers to question and respond to. The response should not seek to commit the other side at this stage. So, 'ah, what you are saying is you are willing to provide more holidays next year' is not recommended. A better approach would be, 'if agreeing more holidays this year for applicability next year is in your mind, I am sure the members would look at that in the light of the whole package'. Or your response to the final example might be: 'If you are saying you recognise the connection between absenteeism levels and domestic childcare difficulties but are concerned about the balance of costs, can I suggest we agree on the principle and work towards agreement on the employer/employee share of the costs.'

Final Offers

Final offers are the most difficult for negotiators to deal with. On the one hand, you have the pressure of members you represent depending on you to deliver the best deal available; on the other, you have the uncertainty of whether what has been offered as the 'final offer' is final, and is the best available. It can frequently be a 'damned if you do and damned if you don't' situation.

If you advise and counsel your member(s) that you have obtained the best settlement possible and at the first sign of sabre-rattling management rush in with an improved offer, you will lose credibility and so will they. For management this could be expensive. If you advise the member(s) to call management's bluff and no improvement is forthcoming or 'the book's not worth the candle', you will look equally incompetent. The abuse of the 'final offer' is, unfortunately, a perpetual occupational hazard for union negotiators.

One distinction to be made at this point is that this dilemma is less acute where the negotiation is more of an integrative and joint-problem-solving nature than in adversarial/conflict negotiations. Here the parties are more open in their approach to sharing information and less likely to be working to inflexible deadlines.

The final difficulty for union negotiators is one that overlaps all aspects of negotiations and it is that union–management negotiations are not only a human and institutional relationship, they are also power relationships. As such, if one party misjudges the power position, of the other or their willingness and ability to exert that position then judgements about the finality of offers can be seriously flawed.

Fictional Case Study: Misreading Signals

A young cavalry officer felt proud when his more experienced colonel left him in charge of the troop for the night. Before returning to the fort for the night, the colonel's last warning was that the Indians camped nearby were of unreliable friendliness and he should use his judgement on whether to post extra sentries around the troop camp.

On returning the next morning, the colonel was confronted by a scene of devastation. His young officer lay bloodied and close to death. 'What happened here – why didn't you post extra sentries?' 'It didn't seem necessary sir', the young officer replied. 'The Indians seemed so happy – they were up singing and dancing all night.'

DON'T MEMORISE – SUMMARISE

Experienced negotiators from unions and management can recall the embarrassment of attempting to negotiate on an item on which agreement was reached at an earlier session. Either side probably prided themselves that they could memorise what had been agreed or they 'had it written down somewhere'. Modern collective bargaining is too complex for such hit and miss approaches. Even when either side can recall what was previously agreed, versions may differ. The problem can easily be resolved by the lead negotiator simply saying: 'I would like a review of where we've got to.' Someone from either side should then summarise where the negotiations have reached, points agreed and points outstanding.

A natural break-point at which to call for a summary is where you have to provide an interim report to member(s) or a union committee. In this instance a summary of what has been agreed is essential if serious misunderstandings are to be avoided.

Regular summaries are good practice in any case but become essential where negotiations are complex, or where they are multi-item and negotiations have moved back and forwards across the agenda. Additionally, the pace of negotiations or influences from the external environment may make summaries an important ingredient of the process.

An example will serve to explain this further. The surge of interest in and pressure for childcare agreements has faced lead negotiators with complex problems. Childcare agreements are multi-component. Among the matters to be settled are the following. Are the childcare facilities to be workplace/municipal authority/private or a combination? What is to be the employer/parent cost share? What form is this to take – salary supplement, cash transfer, vouchers, etc? Is the scheme to be cash limited? What method is to be used on child selection and priority and age? Add to this the external influences of changing tax regimes and of the legislative requirements and it becomes necessary that the 'Let's consider where we've got to' question gets asked at sufficiently frequent intervals.

Obvious complexity is not the only deciding factor in the use and frequency of summaries and reviews. Inexperienced union negotiators should make it a regular practice: it builds confidence and avoids misunderstandings.

Summarising in Low-Trust Relationships

In low-trust relationships 'loss of face' and 'fear of gloating' emotions are very close to the surface. In such circumstances regular summaries can be used to back-stop any tendency to backtrack. However, in order to shore up the thin durability of such situations, it is sometimes safer and wiser to invite the other side to summarise. This helps to neutralise these emotions as the union side can play down its response. It also removes any suggestion that the union side has been opportunistic in its summary. Equally, if the invitation to summarise is refused or fluffed then the union side can soften its approach by saying 'perhaps it would be helpful if I summarise what we believe you have said up to this point'. By putting it this way, the invitation to contradict is implicit but up-front, therefore what comes after can be listened to in a relaxed and non-threatening manner.

ADJOURNMENTS

There is a responsibility on union lead negotiators to ensure that adjournments are used for the purpose intended and that the union team fully understands that purpose. Frequently, negotiations adjourn because a natural break-point has been reached. Presentations have been made, facts have to be checked, other parties consulted. In other circumstances, adjournments have a tactical purpose and some skill is required in deciding when, or when not, to call for an adjournment. Of course, any member of the union negotiating team, or management, can call for an adjournment but authority lies with the lead negotiators to agree to it. There are three general circumstances in which there may be tactical advantage in calling an adjournment.

1. To take stock, to review progress. What has been agreed or offered, what is still outstanding? Other members of the team may want to comment on the process or a specific new proposal. Or perhaps you may want to consult with the 'specialist' member of the team.
2. On occasions discipline can break down in across-the-table negotiations and the atmosphere becomes fractious and counter-productive with the process about to go into the ditch. A timely adjournment accompanied by some nourishment can work wonders in re-establishing a conducive climate.
3. Adjournments can be a tactical means of avoiding impasse or breakdown. The first two adjournments are essentially union caucuses, in this third type the two lead negotiators may wish to meet away from the negotiating table to

discuss without commitment what it would take to unblock the impasse or if the item causing the difficulty should, by agreement, be temporarily put to one side to allow progress on other items.

The union lead negotiator has to make a judgement about the appropriateness of calling for an adjournment but can do so by simply suggesting a break in order to:

- review where we are;
- consider your offer;
- have a coffee break (code for let things cool off);
- explore a way forward over lunch.

Union lead negotiators should not assume that the rest of the team understand why the adjournment has been called and its purpose. Concentrations may have been broken and they may need it explained to them. One word of warning: if the adjournment is to consider a new offer, don't take ten minutes to reject it and fifty minutes discussing sport or the previous night's TV. Management may get the signal that if you took an hour to consider their offer they are close to agreement.

DEADLINES

Ideally, deadlines should be mutually approved.

'I think we can agree that our target should be to have a new agreement before the expiry of the old one on 1 May.'

'I suggest we keep going till 5 p.m. and then adjourn.'

'Unless we get agreement by next Thursday's board meeting, the deal may have to be re-cast.'

'My union executive is meeting next Wednesday to decide on balloting for strike action on this issue. We would prefer to try and reach agreement before then!'

Deadlines of this sort can give a positive push to negotiations, they can help to focus minds and add legitimate pressure. The management negotiator who says they have a plane/train to catch or other urgent business may simply be trying to transfer the pressure on them to you, or be bluffing. Express a willingness to carry on negotiating with another member of the management team authorised to settle, or suggest an adjournment and rescheduled meeting. In any event do not get bounced into a hasty settlement you could later regret.

SUMMARY AND CHECKLIST FOR FACE-TO-FACE MEETINGS

- You are under no automatic obligation to carry anger and frustration into the negotiation room – try to create a tone and climate conducive to achieving your objective. Regard it as more than a courtesy ritual – develop it as a skill. Make sure the climate you create is durable.
- Your case presentation is the first test of your assertions. Use written notes; be as concise as possible and avoid making every point you can think of or delving into unnecessary complexities.
- If you intend to use some kind of specialist from your team, make sure the other side have prior knowledge and the specialist is briefed on what you want from them.
- When summarising your case, re-state your demand or remedy.
- If you have an agenda of items, consider carefully what tactics you intend to deploy, rearrange the agenda if necessary, prioritise certain items, and judge the strength of argument you need to employ.
- Look for an agreed agenda. Avoid, if you can, forcing contentious issues into fragile negotiating arrangements.
- Develop listening and observing skills.
- Learn how to create movement and fluidity in negotiations. Learn how to ask questions – probe the other side. Avoid team members cutting across you, particularly at this stage.

- Use your probing to unblock any impediments to progress; support and protect your opponents if they make concessions. Do not gloat.
- Learn how to identify an offer – no matter how well screened it might be. Tease it out and find out how much flesh is on it. Bear in mind the different kinds of offer. Or you may want to propose one yourself.
- Once you have an offer, check the validity of what you think you heard: summarise it and feed it back to your opponent.
- In long or complex negotiations, summarise as frequently as the circumstances require it. Avoid losing a concession because you forgot to list it in an aggregate summary.
- Use adjournments wisely. Learn the tactical use of adjournments in helping you to make progress or to avoid acrimony.
- Avoid, where possible, unilaterally imposed deadlines. Imagine how footballers act when their team is one goal up with ten minutes to go. Try to get deadlines mutually agreed.

Case Study: The Over-Eager Beaver

Negotiators have many qualities which come in varying strengths: for example, patience, creativeness and ability to assimilate facts. On the other hand, the most damning tendency any negotiator can possess is an eagerness to please, as illustrated in the example below.

A union negotiator arriving at the scene of a strike of a clothing manufacturing plant employing 300 women was greeted by a tense and perplexed Production Director who explained that the factory was about to receive a visit from the company's largest and most important customer, Marks and Spencer. His plea to the union official was 'find out what the girls want and tell them I'll give it to them. Then ask them to go back to work!' The union officer felt that such an over-eager offer might encourage the formulation of a long shopping list well beyond the original cause of the dispute. She decided to resolve the original grievance and cause of the dispute and obtain a return to work pending negotiation on other outstanding issues.

Case Study: Communications – Don't Over-Prepare

One of Britain's most prominent trade union leaders admits to a gross error in communication over an issue which could have had very serious consequences for thousands of his members and others. Faced with the summary dismissal of a union convenor of one of the union's largest plants, he had to persuade the workforce to support that union convenor of some years' standing by agreeing to strike action. This was against the background of the convenor leading opposition to the company's rationalisation and product strategy, wrapped up in a survival package involving large-scale job losses.

The union's right to have a view about company plans had to be defended. The union also had a strong policy historically of opposing victimisation of their shop stewards. Against this background had to be set the nervousness of the workers about their future and that of the company.

Confronting thousands of workers in a car park with an inefficient public address system, he embarked on a disastrous course in communication by producing a set of complex and interrelating arguments. The result was that the members' normal patience turned into confusion and then into anger directed at the union's position. The union lost credibility and the company won the day. The lesson was: on big occasions, keep it simple!

Case Study: Saucy Devil

A local official of Britain's largest union who went on to become its General Secretary was a pretty tough individual who could carry this quality into negotiations when he felt it necessary. However, on one occasion this led to lasting and recurring embarrassment.

On this occasion he spent the morning negotiating with what appeared to be an equally tough and uncompromising Personnel Director. At the lunch break everyone adjourned to the single status canteen after a bitter morning's negotiation, where he found

himself sitting at lunch directly opposite the Personnel Director
and both were still in a bruising mood. Just then a further awkward
situation arose. As he reached over to find the vinegar bottle to
lace his chips, the Personnel Director grabbed the bottle as well.
Continuing their uncompromising mood, both in silence wrenched
at the bottle. Finally the union officer had his first victory of the
day, he gained possession of the bottle and liberally splashed it
over his chips and thudded it back on the table. Only then did he
realise the bottle wasn't malt vinegar, but Pepsi Cola. Maintaining
a bland expression, he finished every morsel on the plate.

Some fifteen years later, while attending the TUC in Brighton
in the crowded lobby of a very posh hotel, he once again came
face-to-face with his aggressive opponent of that day who loudly
hailed him with the cry 'Hello, Ron, still taking Pepsi on yer chips?'

Case Study: Grave Intervention

A senior official of Britain's engineering union in the London area
held extreme political views and was militant in defence of his
members' interests. He was feared by employers but on one
occasion decided that a major employer's offer on an annual
claim on wages and conditions was so lacking in negotiable
substance that humour with a trace of ridicule was justified.

The employer's response was: 'Well, what we are prepared to
offer is nothing on wages, bonus rates remain the same, no extra
holidays or extra holiday pay, no improvement in sick pay or in
the amount of paid sick leave. However, we do not wish to
appear ungenerous, so we are prepared to increase our Employee
Death Benefit by £5, and that is our final offer.'

Almost immediately there began a chapping sound from
underneath the oak boardroom table used for negotiations. The
management team and union team looked at each other
bewildered by the knocking sound they heard – caused, unknown
to them, by this union official banging impatiently with a coin on
the underside of the boardroom table. Eventually the Personnel
Director spoke up: 'What the hell is that noise?' 'Oh, I know', said
the Engineering Union official, beckoning his ear to the floor, 'it's
one of my deceased members, he wants to know if your paltry offer
is retrospective.'

The lesson: never punish a low offer with ridicule, but if you come across a similar exception, try lacing it with humour.

Case Study: Failure to Communicate

If you are going to use negotiators' jargon, make sure you use it correctly. An inexperienced official lacked a clear understanding of his mandate and submitted a claim for a 'substantial across-the-board increase in wages'. The employer responded by offering 8 per cent across the board. His lower paid members rebelled saying that 'across-the-board' meant the same for everyone – which it does not. What they wanted was a flat-rate increase. Across-the-board tells you who; flat-rate tells you what.

8

Closing Negotiations

You have now taken the negotiations forward to a critical point where you have to decide whether you can close the negotiations because sufficient has been obtained to settle the matter, or to break from negotiations and face the predicament of a failure to agree. In an integrative style of negotiations, where both parties are openly committed to seeking a joint solution, then the approach and style of closing a deal are more mutual and open. In adversarial negotiations, this is less so and can be ritualistic and complex.

This chapter examines the various ways in which negotiations can be closed by either the management or union side in concluding a deal. Alternatively, failure to agree on a deal does not mean a deal is not possible. Other avenues and methods are open to negotiators which may eventually lead to a deal and these are explored in this chapter.

THE CLOSE OF NEGOTIATION

When to stop negotiating can be one of the more difficult judgements to make in the negotiating process. If there has been a succession of improved offers it is often difficult to judge when the 'final' offer is exactly that. This problem is compounded by the general over-use of the 'last and final offer' ultimatum. Lead negotiators often have to make a judgement about whether the statement that 'this has to be my last and final offer' is corporate finality or whether it means 'this is as far as I personally have been authorised to go'.

Three minimal conditions have to be met if a 'final' offer has to have any chance of closing negotiations:

- the offer has to be better than the existing condition;

- the offer has to be credible in relation to the union's original claim or grievance;
- the time of the offer has to be right.

Three seemingly simple conditions, but all three need to be present for the final offer to succeed in closing negotiations.

It has been known, however, for final offers to be judged worse than the existing conditions or even the penultimate offer. Also, an offer can be so ill-timed that it lacks credibility. For example, it is rarely in the interest of either side to try and establish a final offer during an acrimonious and ill-tempered session. Equally, final offers made two hours after a strike vote would have more chance two days before. The credibility of an offer is also determined by how it compares with 'the going rate', precedent, union policy, what seems reasonable in the circumstances.

It is not, therefore, necessary to wander around in the dark playing games of bluff and counter-bluff. There are ways of recognising that negotiations are at their final stage and that the final offer or its proximity has been reached. Three further sources that help you to recognise this are the management negotiating team, your own experience and your own team. The management team have a number of ways in which to indicate the close of negotiations. Among these may be the form in which an improved offer is made, or a change of mood and style in the negotiations. Both are intended to signal that management are seeking final agreement. Similarly, changes can take place in how closing offers are received within your own team. Forms of closing negotiations used by management negotiators are usually from a range of tried and trusted methods. Of these, the most frequent are detailed below.

The Final Offer Close

This is where a final offer is made but is tied to the closing of a deal. Sometimes the manner in which this is done is to concede something which is low cost to the employer, but will be highly valued by the union. Equally, management, by laying emphasis on the 'cost squeezing, digging deep' nature of a relatively low-cost concession, will send clear signals about its finality. It is equally not cynical to say that experienced management negotiators can have had a weather eye open for such an opportunity and its timing.

The way this would normally be done is by management stating firmly that what they are about to concede is linked to and a pre-condition of getting agreement across the whole deal. For example, they might say that, 'on the basis of agreeing now on what is on offer' they are prepared to:

- bring forward the re-training arrangements that will allow new opportunities for your members;
- set up a review committee to examine the problems and facilities relating to childcare;
- consolidate all allowances;
- allow paid time off for your members to meet to discuss and vote on the new deal;
- allow your union representatives time off at our expense to attend training sessions on the new agreement;
- allow reinstatement subject to close and agreed monitoring of your members work performance and further appraisal in three months' time.

Management are unlikely to make such a closing offer completely cold, so you should keep alert for an informal 'testing of the water' at this stage of negotiations.

Listing and Valuation Close

This part of the process involves management negotiators listing in full detail all the concessions they have made during negotiations. Negotiators can often forget the amount of progress they may have made, especially during very lengthy negotiations. As well as listing what has been conceded, they will emphasise the total value of what's on offer in relation to individual members, the cost to the employer, and, at times, the value to the union – 'this is a pace-setting agreement'. The reasoning behind this tactic is that very often when the total deal is listed and evaluated, it is seen in a fresh light. It can seem like a new offer, and can appear closer to the union's position that it did earlier.

Conditional Close

The most frequent conditional close is for management to tie a final concession to a condition that the union recommends acceptance of the whole offer. The management tactic would usually run like this: 'Look, we believe that what we have offered is just, reasonable, and will be acceptable to your members. However, if it will help we could seek authority for one final concession in the area you have put to us. However, to do this we are in no doubt that we would require the union's assurance that were it to be conceded, the union would recommend to its members acceptance of the whole package. Can we therefore have that assurance now? We appreciate you may require an adjournment!'

Another 'conditional' close can mean the introduction of an additional factor by management, which will require on your part concessions of a cost-offsetting nature that will help the financing of a final improvement and meet the union's claim. This can be a useful but hazardous route for both union and management if introduced at a late stage in negotiations. a 'strings attached deal' can look worse than the penultimate offer. Don't snatch defeat from the jaws of victory! If management have this in mind they should at the very least float it at an earlier stage. It is then up to them to note the kind of marker the union puts down to it.

The Put-up or Shut-up Final Offer

This is less complex for the union if seriously intended by management. It usually goes something like this: the union must either accept the offer or else management will close the plant; cancel the contract; relocate the work; de-recognise the union; or impose it anyway. In whatever form it comes, such 'or else' offers, if carried through, can have three adverse effects:

- the union loses credibility as the delivery mechanism for improved conditions at work;
- the employees lose their collective representation at work, or have it seriously weakened;
- the union loses membership.

Either way, the union has a more long-term strategic interest, and the negotiators will be obliged to take advice on whether to accept and fight another day, whether sanctions are possible and can be made effective, and whether sanctions will bring success. So, in simple terms, it is put-up or shut-up time for the union side.

When facing all or any of these management strategies for closing negotiations, you will need to review the objectives of both sides, state firmly and clearly if there is still a wide gap between the parties, or signal to the management team what, based on review and consultation, would settle the matter.

Of course, all of these methods of closing down negotiations have the ring of adversarial negotiations. In many union–management negotiations these are not necessary and the matter is simply concluded on a goodwill basis with both sides accepting that they have worked through the problem and the end has been reached. Where the issue at stake relates to an individual grievance, you are likely to know what would be satisfactory to the individual concerned. In others, it is simply a matter of adjourning the negotiations and putting the final offer to those concerned for ratification.

Union negotiators must regard the close of negotiations as the vital stage. Management are not simply trying to close down the process, they are seeking agreement. It may seem to go without saying that the union negotiator will make it clear if the final offer lacks sufficient credibility. As experience is gained, negotiations are often brought to a close by the union negotiator responding to a management request of 'what will settle it' or by initiating it by saying 'give "x" and you have a deal'.

Precipitive, managerial pressure to 'put it to the members' should not lead to a passive acceptance or acquiescence on your part to that approach. The difficulty that can arise for you as union negotiator is that if your intuitive feelings turn out to be right and the members reject the offer, you may be in a worse position than if you had assertively pressed for a further marginal improvement in the last offer. This is the case for four reasons:

- when negotiations resume, they don't go back to the stage immediately prior to the rejection, they move right back to the justification and argument stage;
- following a rejection, people's aspirations are higher;
- management's last offer may have been close to their ultimate limit;
- the members may have rejected the offer and have raised expectations but have little inclination to place sanctions on the employer.

This kind of dilemma is best avoided by avoiding too early a reference to the members, and pressing harder for an improved 'last' offer. Alternatively, if the employer was trying it on, hoping to get a low offer accepted by the members, they will now know that the mistake will be costly and a significantly improved offer will be necessary to secure agreement. If this is done, the union is likely to lose face with the members.

CHANGES IN TEMPERAMENT AND STYLE IN CLOSING STAGES

Making a final and closing offer, even stated explicitly, is often felt by management to be insufficient to gain acceptance. It is, therefore, frequently accompanied by a change of temperament and style within the negotiations. This can mean:

- issuing a written version of the complete offer and requiring a signature of acceptance from the union;

- avoiding all but the most brisk courtesies and emphasising in verbal and non-verbal form the need to get down to the serious business of completing negotiations;
- expressing abrasively, impatience and disbelief at anyone in the union negotiating team who attempts to continue negotiating;
- kicking all suggestions into touch with closed-ended statements such as 'I think we have covered that point', 'I am sure we could look at that next year' or 'We are confident the deal will be accepted as it stands and there is no need for further improvement.'

Similarly, from within your own union negotiating team there can be indicators as to how close you might be to settling. In adjournments, questions can drift from the previous 'how much?' to the more futuristic 'when will it be paid?'; 'will it be retrospective?'; 'will it be in the pay packets before the holidays?'; 'will the extra holidays apply this year?'. Questions on points of detail generally indicate that the substance is settled. One word of warning: if an undisciplined member of your team starts asking such detail questions prematurely, management will gain the same impression.

More often than not, however, union negotiators have to rely on their own experience and grasp of the possibilities in negotiation and have to make up their mind about settling based on that and what is likely to be acceptable to the members.

THE PREDICAMENT OF FAILURE TO AGREE

In the event of failure to agree, assuming that all procedural stages have been exhuasted, there are a number of options open to negotiators. Which to pursue will depend on the circumstances.

Time

First, you could decide not to do anything but wait and see if, over time, circumstances change. A change of personnel, a more favourable economic outlook, an improved order book, could tip the balance towards you. Alternatively, the employer may at some future point come looking for labour force co-operation in some company or organisational initiative. This may be a more ripe time to re-open the outstanding issue. The tactical use of time and circumstance is a legitimate tool of a union negotiator.

Sanctions

A second option could be to seek to apply sanctions. Two forms of sanctions are available: collective industrial action and legal sanctions.

For over a decade now, British governments have sought to do three things in relation to the application of union sanctions: first, to discredit all forms of decision-making except ballots; second, to curb the circumstances in which collective action can be taken; and third, to introduce scrupulous and draconian rules governing the conduct of ballots. In so doing, they have inadvertently elevated ballots on sanctions to the level of a referendum on the employer's last offer, the legitimacy of which then goes unquestioned. The power of workers' determination has been officially ordained. Of course, there are still employers who try to stop action by getting eminent judges to rule that the union has put a word or comma in the wrong place on the ballot paper, but most unions have contracted-out their balloting procedures and this is less of a worry.

The ballot for action is now firmly embedded in the employer's mind as the legitimate manifestation of the workers' power of determination. Union negotiators do, however, have to consider other power elements of the equation but even 'seeking' to apply sanctions adds pressure in negotiations.

The second form of sanction is the law. Workers in Britain at least have more individual than collective legal rights which thus limits the use of this type of sanction. Nevertheless, in 1992 we witnessed the NUM successfully using the law to force British Coal and the government to postpone its planned pit closure programme for a period and legally enforcing the right to be consulted over redundancy proposals.

The power of legal sanctions does not, however, reside purely on how strong a case you have or how successful you might be in a court or tribunal. Legal proceedings are not liked by employers. They are seen as a form of third-party intervention. They are doubly disliked because they can be invoked at the request of a single party. In addition, legal processes can be slow, uncertain, time-consuming and costly; all of which are seen as challenges to employer power. An employer may have other pressing priorities, or may wish to rationalise the cost of settling and the cost of continuing to oppose. Legal cases tend to attract bad publicity, even successfully defended cases can leave an unpleasant smell in the nostrils of the public, as well as present and potential employees. These influences can bring fresh thinking into the negotiations and stimulate the process of seeking solutions and final agreement.

Conciliation, Mediation, Arbitration

Some procedure agreements specify the circumstances under which third-party procedures of either concilitation, mediation or arbitration are invoked. Many also spell out the responsibilities of the parties particularly under arbitration: for example, whether the parties accept arbitration decisions as binding. Some industries, companies and organisations have their own internal machinery for conciliation, mediation and arbitration; others utilise the facilities of the UK government-funded but independent Advisory, Conciliation and Arbitration Service (ACAS).

Conciliators do not propose solutions. They are there merely to help the parties to reach their own agreement. They do this by clarifying and emphasising the areas of agreement and clearing up any points of misunderstanding and identifying precisely the point of disagreement.

If the process of conciliation moves from that to mediation, then it is normally done with the consent of both parties. Mediators are implicitly given the authority to propose remedies, which moves the process of conciliation to a more positive and constructive phase.

Arbitration in Britain has two dominant forms. In traditional arbitration, the arbiter, after listening to the parties, makes up his or her mind. It is popularly argued that arbiters introduce a mediation factor into their decision, 'splitting the difference' as it is called, thus striking what they judge will be a wise and acceptable compromise. In the more contemporary form of arbitration, called pendulum arbitration, this is not permitted. Pendulum arbitration requires the arbiter to come down in favour of the last offer or the last demand. This places pressures on union negotiators not to look extreme in the eyes of the pendulum arbiter. Crudely, if your members are claiming a 15 per cent increase, and the employer has offered 4.5 per cent, and you feel your members would settle for 7 per cent, you are defeating the purpose in continuing to the end to demand 15 per cent. The 'pendulum' is likely to swing the other way. If circumstances dictate that you must act in this way, you will need a very persuasive and compelling case.

Employers generally do not like third-party intervention in their industrial relations, especially if it can be triggered at the request of one party. But essentially it is because management do not like losing control over their own affairs, although, of course, this is the case for union negotiators as well!

The process can be used for a negative as well as positive purpose. It can be used to frustrate the application of other sanctions, but can bring additional and conclusive pressures on both sides.

SUMMARY

We have looked at the pre-conditions for closing a deal, the four most common methods of closing negotiations, and some of the style and behavioural elements of this part of the process. It is important that you learn these, and learn how to detect when they are being used in a genuine and straight-forward way, as well as how to deploy them yourself.

Remember that the timing of an offer is important. There is no reason why you should not advise your negotiating opponents that an offer timed in a particular way would gain easier acceptance. Equally, as I said earlier, a rush to judgement on an offer can be precipitate and foolhardy.

The over-frequent use of the final offer bluff can lead negotiators to believe naively that it is never seriously intended. This can be a costly mistake if it leads you to reject something you have subsequently to recommend as acceptable – so don't fall into that trap. Make a negotiator's judgement about when the end has come. In doing so, you will gain the respect of not just those you represent but your opponent as well.

A negotiator must be positive about the objectives that have been set. You should not, therefore, be planning for failure; you should, however, have a contingency strategy, in case you are unsuccessful. You should know, broadly, what might be done if you face the predicament of no agreement.

Closing negotiations, like other parts of the process, is not an exact science and you can count on misjudging things on occasion. For the most part, common sense and the relationship you have with your negotiating opponent, or partner if you prefer, will tell you when a particular negotiation is closing. Nevertheless, it remains one of the most difficult skills in negotiations and only improves with practice and experience. To make maximum gain from your experience, you should spend some time after each negotiation reflecting on the approach of yourself and your opposite number in closing the deal.

9

Editing, Ratifying and Implementing the Deal

Frequently the close of negotiations is accompanied by feelings of relief, elation, or just simply caving-in tiredness and reduced concentration levels. This is potentially a point in the process when serious errors can be made. While a deal may have been struck on the basis of a general summary of the offer, your professional responsibility may extend beyond the negotiation to reporting back in greater detail to those you represent. They may see the infrastructure of the deal (that is, the implementation, duration dates, the qualifying conditions, whether the new increase will apply to shift, overtime premiums, etc.) as of equally crucial importance.

This chapter therefore deals with a negotiator's responsibility, directly or indirectly, for editing, ratifying and implementing what has just been negotiated. This can be a matter of checking the detail of how what you have achieved will affect those you represent, but a clear break from the negotiating posture is called for. Equally, up until this part of the process your mind as a negotiator has been focused on what you think is achievable: the process now moves to what others think of what you have achieved.

It is also at this stage that intra-union and intra-group tensions can be at their highest. Negotiators have to deal with representational structures, but these structures can be complex and unwieldy. Delegate bodies consisting of 'one representative from each group', as is common, may themselves be unrepresentative because representation of this sort may not reflect the proportion of a group to the whole. The negotiator's role and approach to resolving these problems is discussed in Chapter 3.

Just as the 'closing' stage of negotiations involves a change of style and mood, becoming terminative, more intense, more curt perhaps, then equally the editing stage should ideally involve a lighter, more open and discursive mood. This is essential in order to signal to the other side that you acknowledge the 'negotiating' phase is over. If you do not do this, the other side may harbour feelings that you are not only editing the deal but still seeking advantage or being opportunistic. At best this may slow the process down, at worst it may encourage similar feelings in the other side – 'ah, what can we trim?'

By adopting a lighter mood and more open style, you encourage an approach that is based on efficiency and mutual interest. In this environment, if misunderstandings do surface then they are more likely to be regarded as genuine rather than based on late opportunism or afterthought. The second advantage this approach has is that whether the deal covers a single member or a group of members, when you report back or counsel, you have the confidence that the information and advice you are giving is soundly based on full and mutual understanding of the terms.

Having adjusted the mood and style for this stage of the process, the next important point is to have as comprehensive a checklist as necessary. Much of what you want to check may have already been referred to in the negotiations. You may have consulted your negotiating team or even more widely, but now is the time to ensure that the how, what, why, when and where is fully understood. This represents the infrastructure of the deal, essentially it is this that makes the deal hang together.

In the case of large employer organisations with personnel human resource departments, this checking phase may coincide or closely precede the preparation and issuing of a written agreement, or in some cases simply a letter. Alternatively, agreement drafting skills are something you are unlikely to find among small and medium-size companies. In these circumstances, verbal reiteration and note-taking may have to be relied upon. The union side could volunteer to draft the agreement itself, although instances of this are rare. Most managements would be apprehensive about devolving that responsibility to a union, fearing not necessarily duplicity in the drafting, but nuance, emphasis, sequence and precision.

Editing for equality implementation is another crucial part of this stage. Negotiators in most countries now have a responsibility legally or professionally to negotiate equality of treatment, regardless of gender, race and, increasingly, sexual orientation. Editing negotiation outcomes is about more than the principles, it is also dependent on information that those affected by the deal bring to those responsible for editing and ratifying the deal, about the deal's impact on different groups of members.

MISUNDERSTANDINGS AT THE CHECKING, DRAFTING STAGE

What marks this stage of the negotiation process as vitally important is that the time, effort and creativity of both sides can quickly be dissipated if misunderstandings or erroneous conclusions are not identified at this stage. Genuine and quite innocent misunderstandings can arise from either side. People, even experienced negotiators, can genuinely believe that something has been agreed when it has not.

So what should be done if such a problem should arise at this very late stage? That depends on who is on the deficit side of misunderstanding. If the management is on the 'losing' side of it and it is not too costly, they may concede the point; if they do not, you never had it anyway and you are back into negotiation. If, on the other hand, the deficit is on the union side, you have to ask two questions. Is the deficit point sufficient to withdraw overall agreement? If not, what more can be done? If the former is the case then sensibly you are back into negotiation; if the latter, you have to judge whether to make an issue of it at this very late stage. If you judge you are unlikely to be successful, then management may respect you for letting the point slide rather than creating the impression that it is a bad or deficient negotiated outcome.

What you should not do is go for the 'five hundred mile fudge'. The clarity and accuracy of the terms of an agreement should never be a function of the proximity of the negotiators to the place of implementation. Leaving it to someone else to sort out with fudged wording is not only neglectful and unprofessional, it could be costly for the union and employer if a strike results from it.

RATIFICATION AND IMPLEMENTATION

Clearly the two things are connected. Without ratification there can be no mutually agreed implementation. Ratification meetings and presentations, whether related to a personal or collective issue, should confirm who is covered, how they will be affected, when the agreement will apply, what it contains, why settlement is being recommended, and so forth. The ratification explanation should also reflect the context of the negotiations and explain the process. If the deal has strings or conditions attached, then you may feel they should be fed into the ratification process in the same way as they are likely to have been put to you – conditions first, concessions second. But there are no rule for this!

Ratification meetings are for a positive purpose, they are for the members to arrive at a collective view on whether what is on offer is acceptable. They should not consist of a listing of 'all the things we failed to achieve'. Negative report-backs signal that no agreement is better than what is on offer. If that is not what you are saying, you are confusing your audience. If you are seeking ratification of your efforts and final outcome, your responsibility is to be positive but balanced in your presentation. Explaining how tough negotiations have been is acceptable. Overdoing it can sound like a plea of mitigation for bringing forward a weak agreement.

Implementation of agreements is largely but not wholly a managerial responsibility. During the ratification process you will have covered what will be implemented and when. However, for negotiators, honouring the implementation extends beyond this. Members can react when they see the detail of an agreement and how it affects them. This is particularly so where the agreement involving work organisation changes and where misunderstandings may easily occur. Equally, local management and supervision can become over-enthusiastic, even opportunist, about what a new agreement permits.

Negotiators in these circumstances often have to reach beyond the letter of the agreement back to what each side said to each other across the table. These residual responsibilities of a negotiator can be crucial in bedding in an agreement. How honourable you are seen to be might shape what you are offered in the future. Backtracking has its own long-term downside.

10

Venues, Facilities, Time, Communications

This is a general chapter covering a range of matters which I think of as the furnishings and fittings of negotiations. Venues, facilities, time and communications, while not perceived as the 'meat' of the negotiating process, can nevertheless be conducive or otherwise to the efficient conduct of negotiations.

VENUE

The venue for union–management negotiations is most commonly on the employer's premises or those of an employers' association, but occasionally a neutral venue is preferred by either side. Unless there is a specific reason, most union negotiators have no objection to negotiations taking place on employers' premises. This is so for a number of reasons: it is usually convenient, allows easy and ready access to information, documentation, interested parties, and most importantly, if the employer is hosting they usually do not mind providing food and refreshments, if needed. Lastly, employers' premises are places where meetings of other kinds take place and are therefore likely to have suitably sized rooms and facilities.

When a preference is expressed for a neutral venue, perhaps a hotel/conference suite, union negotiators must bear in mind that they may have to secure from the union the resources to act and respond independently in relation to the venue arrangements.

Management may be willing to pay the hire costs of a meeting room, but not the costs of a union side-room, nor meals and refreshments. The cost of coffee and sandwiches,

132

meals, and overnights can soon mount in expensive hotels, so do not find yourself embarrassed – get authority to fund your side of the business if that is necessary.

Case Study: The Host That Turned

A major American company conducted minor negotiations in-plant, but annual pay negotiations and other major matters were conducted in neutral territory, usually hotels, and fully hosted by them. However, during a particularly difficult strike a meeting was arranged by the company in a large city-centre hotel some 25 miles from the plant. The union officers arrived, assuming wrongly that the usual courtesies would be extended. What they found was that the company, in a belligerent mood, had hired a cleared small bedroom on the 10th floor to meet the union officers. The room was too small, deliberately so, to permit the shop stewards to attend the negotiations. The Shop Stewards Committee was left sitting in the public reception areas, no side-room, no refreshments. The union officers also found going up and down ten floors in the lift every time an adjournment was necessary somewhat inconvenient. After several hours, as hunger and tiredness set in, the union side began to realise the difficulty of their position. Twenty-five miles from home base, no proper transport arrangements, no food or money and a management insistent that negotiations continue. Lessons were learned!

Where a venue is long-established, tried and tested as a place for negotiations, then the parties will have sorted out the basic essentials required for formal negotiations. Where a new or alternative venue is being used or established then ideally you are looking for the following facilities.

A Negotiating Room

You will need a room or office of such a size that it can comfortably accommodate both the union and management negotiating team. On a permanent site this may mean designating both a small to medium-size office or room for certain negotiating meetings and perhaps a larger one for more formal and complex negotiations involving an expanded 'team' on either side. Room size is important, it is not conducive to the resolution of conflict to be sat at either end of an 18-foot boardroom table with pitched voices echoing round the room in a seemingly confrontational manner.

An Ante-room

You will also need an ante-room where side-meetings during adjournments can be held. 'Adjourning to the canteen' is not always a good idea: there can be too many distractions and time-wasting.

Seating arrangements for negotiations is a subject that excites and intrigues psychologists. More so since the American/Vietnam peace talks in Paris where reputedly several weeks were spent discussing the seating arrangements to prevent either side gaining psychological advantage. Trade union negotiations have no need to over-concern themselves with the shape of the seating arrangements and psycho-advantage. Most union negotiators are comfortable with across-the-table type of arrangements. This has as much to do with practicality as the psychology of the two sides approach. As a union negotiator, when you walk into a room you want to know who is who, and keep your own side close to you for consultation and back-up.

One union officer hurriedly arriving for a plant negotiation sat down and in hushed tones relayed to the Personnel Manager's secretary the inherent weaknesses in the equal pay case he was there to argue, mistaking her for the staff union representative because she was sitting on the 'wrong' side of the table.

Where the issues under negotiation call for a more integrative and problem-solving approach, many negotiators, union and management, feel that a less formal, more relaxed, non-sided seating arrangement is conducive.

Telephone, Photocopying and Fax Facilities

These are now essentials for the efficient conduct of negotiations. Where new proposals are being tabled, it is essential that all of the negotiating team are given copies as soon as practical. One note of caution: the lead negotiator needs to control the status of printed pre-produced matter and its circulation. Panic can set in with the circulation of a crude and unnegotiated management proposal. Fax facilities are fast becoming invaluable in multi-worksite negotiations. Opinions can be quickly sought on amended proposals, thus avoiding the need to re-call expensive regional or national meetings.

Food and Refreshments

These are the necessary fuel for sustaining negotiations. They can also be used as 'reward' for intensive effort, or a stress-release mechanism. Carrying on too long without a break and physical sustenance can lead to an unnecessary increase in tension. It is amazing what changes in atmosphere can take place on resuming after a coffee and sandwich break. Equally, 'let's carry on and crack this problem before we break for food' can be a motivator. But don't fall into the trap of exchanging a bad deal for a steak lunch.

Finally, where the employer is hosting negotiations they will normally lay on the food and refreshments. However, they are not mindreaders. If negotiations are multi-site, the union side will have to detail what facilities will be required for visiting representatives and full-time officers, including timings.

A postscript on food and refreshments. Macho negotiators who tell you they can lace the tension and complexity of negotiations with the consumption of alcohol are simply deluding themselves. Union representatives who are perhaps on the fringe of the negotiating team may feel they can afford the luxury of a tipple, the lead negotiator and core team most definitely cannot. Breaking open the cocktail cabinet if felt necessary should be held over as a purely 'signing celebration' – if the deal you have done warrants it!

TIME AND UNION NEGOTIATORS

Time used wisely in negotiations can mean power. The employer who strings out negotiations and delays settling when you have a strong and sound case is transferring power to the union. Members will commit themselves more strongly to their claim and channel their anger and frustration towards the employer. Conversely, if the employer is expecting circumstances to change, the transference may be of temporary advantage and the union may have to force the pace or watch their position weaken.

This is particularly vivid in pay negotiations, where management may observe that the rise in the average earnings index or Retail Price Index is dropping and hence delay in settling will make the union's claim less publicly credible. A useful management tactic! – the reverse, of course, is equally true. The point to be learned is that union negotiators frequently have to keep an eye on external and public issues which can very quickly overtake their negotiating position and tactics.

To have a long list of unresolved or partially resolved issues in the queue for attention is bad for industrial relations and therefore bad for the union. However, there can be genuine reasons for delaying the resolution of an issue. One is where settlement with one group may have a knock-on effect and lead to consequential claims by other groups. In these circumstances some delay by management in dealing with the issue is often, though not invariably, justified. Some pacing in these cases may allow time for the union to alter tactics, or for the 'consequential groups' to cool their heels.

Timing within particular negotiating sessions is also important. Reference was made earlier to attention span and case presentation. You should get your key points over in the first 3–5 minutes maximum and ideally your whole opening presentation, if it is a formal one, should not extend beyond 10–15 minutes. Whole negotiating sessions are best limited to around two hours. Too long sessions affect accuracy, creative ability, and thereby efficiency. Inexperienced negotiators make the frequent mistake of believing that pressure and intensity is all, but calling an adjournment can often bring new energies and initiatives to the table.

COMMUNICATIONS

Telephones

Most trade union negotiators would freely admit that pressure and pace of work compel them to over-use the telephone. But when pressure and circumstances, rather than choice and judgement, dictate how you do something, the risks of error are higher. Negotiating by telephone has advantages, disadvantages and limitations, and is worthy of a brief mention.

Telephone negotiation is of course still a two-way verbal communication. But it differs from face-to-face negotiation in certain obvious and other less obvious ways. Essentially, the telephone although two-way is only a one-to-one communication. There is also an absence of body language and that does sometimes require you to be more explicit than you otherwise might have been. Because of this, open 'voice boxes' attached to telephones can sound harsher than the caller intended. The ethical use of voice boxes is to advise the other party that they are now on open communication and, most importantly, who else is in the room at any point in the conversation. But beware, not everyone is ethical to that degree.

Telephone negotiations are most useful in dealing with preliminaries and matters of detail but should be approached in the same way as face-to-face negotiations by asking 'what are my objectives here?':

- am I looking to settle this?
- to simply clarify matters?
- to pacify and sort out misunderstandings?
- to use the opportunity to get into a negotiating position?
- to simply sort out the next stage?

Three things should be avoided in telephone negotiations: aggression, thorny issues and complexity. Aggression can be halted by the other side hanging up – if a bit of humility is required in order to repair relationships, the party at fault is disadvantaged. When this kind of thing occurs it is better to withdraw regardless of what your emotions urge you to do.

People who end telephone conversations on a fractious note invariably still have residual strains of it at subsequent meetings. Failure to repair these prior to a meeting can impede agreement. Always try to end on a positive note such as 'we can take this further when we meet' or 'there will be a better opportunity later'. Thorny issues are best left to face-to-face meetings unless you want simply to put out soft feelers. 'I know this is a difficult one and I thought I would find out how you feel before we meet.'

Complexity is to be avoided. Keep it simple. Expecting the receiver to hold complex facts, figures and arguments in their head will make them feel at a disadvantage and they will recoil. If a face-to-face meeting is not possible or desirable then it is best to advise the other side that you wish to cover your general area of concern and will follow up with more detail in a fax or letter.

Tactically speaking, the telephone can be a problem. Elsewhere in this text I cautioned about getting bounced in negotiations. There is something about the telephone that induces otherwise guarded people to drop their guard and respond quicker than they might otherwise. Perhaps it is prioritising under pressure, perhaps when body language is absent their power persona changes, perhaps their perception of power relativities leads them to believe that an impatient 'Yes, Yes, – I'll speak to you later' means 'Yes – but if I change my mind later I can reverse my decision.'

Prioritising under pressure comes with the portfolio of union negotiators, as does getting simple matters sorted out that someone otherwise might spend hours picking over. It is, however, a skill. Prioritising means you are in control. Getting pushed means someone else is. If in doubt, delay, call for more information. Bad decisions made in a hurry usually come back to visit you.

Letters

Correspondence by letter or fax can make an important contribution to the negotiating process. It is not simply a substitute for verbal communication as it offers different advantages to face-to-face or telephone communication. A single letter represents an opportunity for a one-sided and uninterrupted communication. By its virtue it lets you put your own point of view as well as what you perceive to be that of the other side, without interruption, or an immediate countering response. Linked to the fact that it is a permanent record to which repeated references can be made, it permits more accurate reference to other parties – and if necessary allows the point to sink in. Its advantage over the telephone is that it is a better medium through which more complex information can be carried. You can make your communication multi-channelled by sending copies to whosoever you choose, although over-use of this practice can be discourteous and counter-productive.

The downside to the written word is that it can look more strident and aggressive than verbal communication. A blunt accusation made face-to-face can be softened by appropriate body language. In the written form it just sits there. Other disadvantages to be considered when using written communication is that it is a form of open communication and you may disclose too much. You may also find that events have overtaken you by the time your correspondence is read.

Like other elements of the process, negotiating in the written word is a skill to be developed. Its uses are limited and so must your objectives be in using it. You can use it to explain and clarify your position and counter-pose that of your opponents. You can use it to shape attitudes, create a conducive climate for a forthcoming face-to-face meeting. You may even use it to put yourself in a negotiating position when you get there.

One final word: negotiating correspondence calls for absolute accuracy. You have now temporarily seconded your secretarial staff on to your 'team', but you are responsible for what is said. Ghastly errors can occur. Transposing from notes, tapes or shorthand may pass through two or three sets of hands but its accuracy is your responsibility. If not, your objective may be foiled and misunderstandings arise.

Faxes

A few points about faxes as an alternative to letters. First, they are a more open form of correspondence and may be seen by more people. Second, they are intended for something more urgent than first-class post. Non-urgent faxes arriving in the middle of the day are an irritating attempt to transfer your urgency or impatience on to someone else and will be seen as that. Thirdly, they may miss completely routine consideration and allocation of correspondence.

The key advantage of faxes is, of course, speed combined with accuracy. During negotiations documents can be quickly sent to multi-site workplaces for quick consultations, and meetings can be arranged more rapidly. I do think it is inadvisable to use faxes when dealing with personal cases, they are frequently confidential and faxes are not.

SUMMARY

Venues and meeting facilities are often taken for granted and in most cases the employer will provide them. However, you do need to ensure the adequacy of them. We discussed in Chapter 2 the issue of the underlying attitude of management negotiators to the negotiating process. One way you will recall of limiting the functioning of the union is to deny the facilities for negotiating meetings to them. The matter does need careful attention and lay representatives need to tackle any limiting actions of this sort.

Similarly, with a 'hostile' employer, meetings are normally pre-arranged to be brusque and short. It is sensible in these situations to be as comprehensively prepared as possible. With 'hostile' employers, written pre-notification and an outline of agenda items can be a useful tactic.

It is always difficult to estimate how long a negotiating meeting will last. However, a brief outline and key points should be aimed for. If a meeting is simply going round in circles, you are wasting time and a break for coffee or a complete adjournment may be best.

Using telephones to deal with complex or thorny issues is best avoided. Aggression by either side should, if it occurs, be repaired before ending the call.

Written communication offers a one-way method of getting your point over and having a written record if you think you will need it at a later date. The written word should always be courteous. Blunt or accusatory statements look awful in print and will only get the other side's hackles up and provide a diversion from the point at issue. The same point can be made about faxes, except they are an even more open medium of communication. Faxing letters that contain personal information given in confidence should be avoided and not done without the person's permission.

Telephones, faxes and letters offer additional tools to the negotiator. On rare occasions they can substitute for face-to-face meetings but for the most part they are a helpful supplement to the negotiating process. Negotiators must develop the necessary skills in knowing how best to exploit their opportunities and avoid their pitfalls.

11

Negotiators and the Law

Labour law in most countries tries to balance the interests of labour and capital. The extent to which that balance weighs in favour of one side is dependent on the political hue of a country over time. Rarely, other than in what was the Eastern Bloc, has it weighed in favour of labour. The experiences and attitudes in this chapter, although drawn from UK law, are shared by negotiators more widely. The reader should not expect a chapter about the law, rather it is about negotiators' attitudes towards the law, its historical position in regulating relations at work and its tactical use in negotiations.

NEGOTIATORS' ATTITUDES TO THE LAW

Most negotiators have ambivalent, almost schizophrenic, feelings about the intrusions of the law in the negotiating process. They suffer from a sense of frustration, partly due to the 'third party' intervention factor and partly from its legendary inadequacy as an agent of worker protection. Primarily, however, these feelings arise from the fact that frequently weak and biased judicial standards are used to settle differences that negotiators would prefer, in this context, to see settled through the power relationship. Compounding this frustration is the mistaken high expectation that working people have of the law in employment. However, when legal realities leave them feeling short-changed, their residual feelings of injustice turn them towards their union negotiators to extract their 'rights'.

Three examples will illustrate facets of British employment legislation:

1. In the UK, 75 per cent of applicants taking their sense of injustice to an industrial tribunal lose their case; even the 25 per cent who do win are frequently penalised for petty elements of 'contributory fault'.

2. The law of contract has for over one hundred years been distorted by the judiciary when applied to employment contracts. Contracts are principally agreements freely entered into and mutually agreed. Yet when it comes to employment contracts, the law has historically permitted employers to make unilateral changes to employment contracts, using a number of judicial devices. In the UK, in the *Rigsby* v. *Ferodo* (1991) case, the judiciary permitted damages to be paid for unilaterally imposed changes in Rigsby's contract. They then, however, generously offered to employers a means by which they could avoid this difficulty in the future.

3. As regards the laws on equality, it is disheartening that so many have been short-changed for so long by so few. Union negotiators of wiser counsel have watched in anguish as the high hopes of women have been dashed by the introduction of a series of deliberately weak and over-complex legislation on equality.

The three examples above are not offered to create in the reader's mind a totally negative view of the intrusion of the law itself into the negotiating process. Laws are necessary. But everything in the employment relationship cannot be resolved through a judicial process. The examples given are intended to illustrate that in Britain the relationship between the law and union negotiators is a troubled one. It sits uneasily on the shoulders of union negotiators. In Europe and other areas of the industrial world it may be different, but I suspect not. Nevertheless, within this setting negotiators require a command of the law relevant in the employment relationship.

There is a vast list of legal provisions of potential interest to negotiators. Learning this would be a daunting but unnecessary task. A good working knowledge of the core legislation impacting on those you negotiate for is, however, essential, as well as general and occupationally specific legal jurisdiction.

Unlike other countries, Britain with certain minimal exceptions does not have laws that act as props to the process of collective bargaining. Italian and French workers have a legal right to join a trade union, to organise and to take strike action. Swedish, French and American employers (with certain caveats) are legally obliged to bargain in good faith with unions. The exceptions in Britain are certain pieces of legislation derived from the European Union requiring consultation with unions over large redundancies and in cases involving the transfer of a business. Worker-elected safety representatives in Britain also have, on specified matters, a right to be consulted. The UK government recently removed from statute the responsibility of the Advisory, Conciliation and Arbitration Service (ACAS) to promote collective bargaining as a means of resolving conflict in industrial relations. Other proposals within the European Union designed to extend consultation rights have either been vetoed by the British government, dropped because of British attrition, or opted out of by Britain as in the social policy protocol of the 1992 Maastricht Treaty.

So the UK law does little to prop up the negotiating process. But what role does it play in the negotiating interface between unions, employers and employees? To make sense of the law's role in negotiation and make progress in understanding negotiators' use of the law, we can say that the law purports to do four broad things. It tries to influence the behaviour of the parties by seeking to provide a basis for

- fair treatment in employment;
- equal treatment in employment;
- a safe working environment;
- constraining and regulating the ability of unions to introduce sanctions.

But fairness and equality are loose concepts. Wide gulfs exist between the providers and the beneficiaries of the standards set down within these concepts. One has only to consider how short-changed women in many countries feel over equality laws to realise that the law is but one factor in relations at work and that negotiators need to learn when and how to use it.

TACTICAL CONSIDERATIONS

The law operates essentially as a secondary means of settling differences. Properly employed, it assists the process of negotiations in important respects, and replaces it only in the final resort. In most countries the law offers a framework of rules and standards ostensibly on fair and equal treatment against which negotiations take place. These rules operate directly over a wide spectrum of negotiating issues (equal opportunities, pensions, discipline, discrimination, redundancy, health and safety, maternity) and form the indirect background against which other negotiations take place (retirement arrangements, promotion procedures, training, compensation packages, etc.). It is impossible for any trade union negotiator to ignore them. Outside obviously quantifiable questions such as the length of notice rights, the amount of maternity or redundancy pay, the law establishes few objectively measurable standards. So it is not the case, as was fashionable to assert in the 1970s, that the law is best regarded as setting a 'floor of rights', on top of which trade union negotiators can consciously and conscientiously erect a mansion of enhanced entitlements. Viewing the law as a structure, which offers a rough shelter for the weak and houses the well-organised to a better standard is not an outlook which helps the negotiators. It inclines the negotiator to see the law as an output rather than as an input, as a menu rather than as an ingredient.

This outlook suggests that the law is a fixed and solid edifice of facts which should be asserted as such. There will, of course, be situations where legal entitlements themselves are the subject of disagreement: for example, where under UK law an employer refused to pay full pay to an employee on sick leave while under statutory notice, or where an employer makes an unauthorised deduction from pay. In such circumstances there is little alternative but to assert what the law is, and insist that members' rights are observed. But this is hardly the stuff of negotiations. When the law acts as policeman, the emphasis is upon application – where a policing role is invoked the scope for agreement and discussion is limited.

In negotiations which do not directly involve the enforcement of legal entitlements as such, the real questions to be considered are whether legal standards will assist in progressing the negotiations at some stage and how the law can be used to best advantage in attaining the objectives which have been set. This outlook does not view the law as a structure, but as a tool or factor in advancing discussion towards agreement.

In situations where the law is relevant it is essential to consider what effect raising legal considerations will have. Legal objections can be used to seal or block off certain areas of discussion. This can also happen inadvertently if the other party is unsure of the territory over which they are being invited to tread. Ignorance of the law is frequently an excuse for defensive behaviour. The possibility of legal difficulties in one direction can also induce people to look for other directions in which to move. Legal standards can sometimes form a useful starting point from which to develop negotiating positions. Using the law in negotiations is, therefore, a tactical question rather than a matter of principle.

Consider a situation, for example, in which organisational change results in changed skill requirements. There could be enhanced opportunities in new skill areas, different demands may be made in these jobs. There may be a reduced need for skills in other areas, making members employed in those jobs potentially surplus to requirements. The legal issues involved are complex. Are the workers employed in surplus areas technically redundant? Does one of the tenets of redundancy apply that 'the requirements of the business for work of a particular kind has ... diminished'? If so, is there a legal requirement for potentially surplus staff to be offered the alternative work which is available? What happens if they are forced to apply for different jobs, and fail the interview? Will the dismissal be unfair if they are subsequently dismissed? If not, do staff have the right to refuse the new jobs when offered? Can they be compulsorily transferred to the new work? What is their legal right to refuse to move? And what happens if they do move into new skill areas and are not up to the new demands of the job? What obligations does the employer have if there is a substantial loss of bonus earnings while they progress along the learning curve? These are all interesting legal questions.

The negotiating agenda will be very different. It is likely that negotiations will aim to achieve the best available options for the staff affected by organisational change. It will be looking to avoid compulsory redundancies, although voluntary redundancy may be more acceptable to some staff than the uncertainty of job change. Existing staff will look to be given prior consideration over external candidates in relation to new opportunities. Access to training in the new skills will be a priority. Precautions will need to be taken to ensure that the effect of job change does not disadvantage women or ethnic minorities. Maintenance of earnings will be another key priority. Potentially surplus staff will need assurances about their future – inside the company through future work guarantees, or perhaps outside by guarantees covering rights to anticipate notice of redundancy without prejudice to redundancy and notice entitlements. In situations like this, negotiators need to consider how the law best advances progress towards the objectives set for negotiations. If the employer is trying to force the pace, and is inclined to pay little attention to members' interests, how can the law be used to slow the pace down, and concentrate the employer's mind on the needs of the staff with existing skills? Can the legal questions concentrate their attention on their obligations towards their staff whose skills they no longer need in such numbers? Can retraining be introduced as a right, rather than as an unaffordable luxury? The law in these circumstances will be used as a lever to inch a boulder of discussion towards agreement.

THE INFORMATION LOOP

Negotiation is based upon information – or, rather, around the lack of it. There would be no real scope for negotiation if both sides possessed perfect information about the other. Consider, for example, a situation where a prospective buyer and prospective seller of a second-hand car both knew exactly what condition it was in; both had full information about their respective need to buy and sell; as well as the price at which the other party was prepared to settle. In such circumstances, the need for negotiation would be very circumscribed, and would only involve other variables.

The information loop in negotiations is formed from four sources: from the members themselves, from the employer, from the negotiator's personal knowledge, and from the research and collation of the negotiator. So some information comes from within the loop formed by the two negotiators, and some is fed into the loop from external sources.

The law acts in three different ways in the dynamics of the loop: first, the law itself, both statutory and common, is a source of information; second, the law furnishes unions and individuals with the right of access to certain types of information; and third, the law provides sanctions for refusal to divulge information in defined areas.

Union negotiators are not lawyers, nor should they be. However, they should have a working knowledge of the relevant Statutes, Regulations, Codes of Practice, and Guidance Notes which exist. Periodic reference to case law keeps negotiators informed of how and in which direction the law is moving. This can be particularly important with new legislation where it is expected that the 'law' will be in a developmental stage for a period of time. The equality laws have been a case in point. The purpose of establishing the relevance and usefulness of the law in the information loop is twofold. It can be used to counsel the member(s) and/or employer or, alternatively, to contest the other side's case. But the law turns on the facts of a case as much as points of law. Negotiators should always have an eye to what rights the law provides on access to information. Apart from what effect it may have on the substance of the case, it can inform negotiators tactically on what information should be sought prior to a meeting or during it. See Chapter 6 on the importance of preparation.

EQUALITY AND THE LAW

Seeking fair and equal treatment may seem the natural constituency of unions, universally acknowledged and accepted. However, it continues to be an area of evolutionary social development as well as legal change. Negotiators have to strive to maintain an unambiguous position against a background of changing social attitudes, the development of economic and political power of previously discriminated groups, and the impact of all of this on power and employment relations at work. It is arguable that in most developed countries, equality has become the dominant area of the law governing the behaviour of negotiators.

Fair treatment is principally related to natural justice. The right not to be unfairly dismissed, the right to a hearing and proper procedures consistently applied, the right to be consulted and access to external appeal bodies. Equal treatment legislation, on the other hand, while containing requirements about conduct, is principally an economic issue.

The differences between race and gender in this sense are simply ones of proportion and cultural history rather than principle. There are more women than ethnic minority men in the labour force and they have been denied equal treatment for a historically longer period. Ethnic women are liable to suffer dual discrimination.

The role of the union negotiator in relation to equality is not a negative one. You are not there simply to stop or prevent inequality or discrimination. The responsibility of union negotiators is to be fully cognisant with the principles and practices of equality legislation and to positively seek their implementation. Here again a useful working knowledge and update can be obtained by reference to the Codes of Practice on Race, Sex and the UK Periodic Guide to Case Law produced by the Industrial Relations Law Reports and Equal Opportunities Review.

Case Study: What's in a Day

After a prolonged bitter strike a small residue of strikers refused to return to work on the due date. Bitter at the terms of settlement, they vowed to 'stick it out'. They amounted to twelve out of an original two hundred strikers and refused to listen to union advice about returning to work.

The company's patience wore thin and they wrote to each person stating that unless they returned to work on a given date they would be regarded as having terminated their own employment. Seven returned to work on the date set by the employer. Five phoned the company on that morning to say they were now on sick leave. The union advised that if this was genuinely the case they should submit a doctor's certificate immediately. Still in a defiant mood they retorted that their collective agreement gave them five days to submit a certificate.

Their advised day of return was a Thursday and on the following Monday evening hand-delivered letters informed them of their dismissal. On the following morning (Tuesday) the company found doctor's certificates delivered to them.

All five appealed to an Industrial Tribunal claiming unfair dismissal on the grounds that their agreement gave them five days to submit a certificate and the company had sacked them inside that period.

The Tribunal accepted that the workers genuinely thought the agreement meant five 'working days', but it didn't say that. The Tribunal had to rely upon the Interpretation Act (1897) and found that 'days' meant 'calendar days'. This included Saturday and Sunday. The dismissal was therefore fair.

Case Study: Embarrassing Citable Behaviour

A young Asian assistant manager was subjected to repeated remarks about his colour and racial origins from his senior manager. He felt he was being subjected to racial abuse and discrimination by the senior manager. After suffering this for several months he was sacked without good reason or representation. His union pressed the company to admit racial discrimination and reinstate him, but they refused. A Tribunal heard evidence of the senior manager's racist conduct and subsequently found in the young Asian's favour, citing racial discrimination as the reason for his dismissal. The union negotiated a five-figure sum of compensation in out-of-court settlement. The food chainstore is still counting the loss of business from the Asian and wider community following the Tribunal publicity.

SUMMARY

For negotiators the law is a tool. Where workers have individual or collective rights, negotiators must have a thorough working knowledge of them. Similarly, if the law intervenes in the negotiating process or the union's ability and efficiency in introducing sanctions, then negotiators must be aware of this.

However, the use of the law is essentially a tactical decision. You should consider: 'Will I, by invoking the law, move matters closer to my negotiating objective?' If all other considerations such as cost, timing, or wider ramifications, do not override, then you may wish to proceed. If all you seem to be doing is proving a legal point, you should reconsider.

On equal treatment, the position of negotiators must be unambiguous. Union negotiators cannot by action or implication be judged to have supported discriminatory deals. On behaviour they have to be firmly on the side of the harassed and not an appellant harasser. In the UK, legislation and supporting Codes of Practice by implication oblige negotiators to negotiate in a manner that observes the standards of equal treatment.

No matter how ambivalent negotiators feel towards the law in employment, particularly during a period of rapid change at work, the law can be a useful tool to have. It can be used to obtain information, to block a line of action or enquiry, to embarrass or harass. It does, though, remain a secondary means of resolving conflict at work and is therefore only an ingredient in most cases and not a complete answer.

12

Conclusions

Most people who negotiate have other responsibilities in their occupation or profession. They are administrators, people managers, technicians, for part of their time and negotiators for other parts. So most negotiators are required to move into and out of a negotiations mode.

Having read through the preceding chapters, the reader will readily appreciate that switching into negotiators' mode means switching into a behavioural and attitudinal mode in addition to turning on a whole range of negotiators' skills. You will also have learned that the behavioural and attitudinal mode is controlled less by natural inclination and more directed by the need to advance towards an objective. Negotiators' skills training is important: research skills, case analysis and presentation skills all require formal training. Listening, questioning and observational skills can easily be supplemented by some self-training techniques. Reviewing what you did and how you did it against a checklist is a good way of deepening and strengthening these skills. Self-control over a simple tendency or impulse to butt in on the other side can easily be achieved by a practical effort to curb it.

In the field of industrial relations union negotiators are held accountable in ways less applicable to others. Democratic pressures from below and hierarchical pressures from above are often in conflict as some of the earlier quoted case studies reflect. These pressures form one of the most important impacts on the quality of relationship between union negotiators and those they represent. These intra-organisational tensions extend the negotiator's role into the wider context of the negotiating process and involve the application of negotiating and communication skills in the resolution of intra-union and intra-group conflict. Different approaches are required to this aspect of the process. There is no preferred or guaranteed

152

approach. Trying either of the approaches described or depending on your own natural tendency is as good a guide as any.

The assessment of power can in some negotiating situations be no more than a recognition of the self-evident; in others it can be more complex. It may even, as suggested, change over the relevant time period. This is no exact science but it is essential that negotiators comprehend the elements and levers of power in any given situation.

Planning and preparation are the essential prerequisites of any successful negotiations. The starting point has to be a joint acceptance by both sides, first that there is an issue to be jointly resolved and, second, that the authorisation and willingness to do so through negotiation exists. Without this, a successful outcome is never in sight and any progress towards it is likely to be frustratingly slow. Removing the obstacle to progress is a tactical challenge for negotiators. The passage of time and a changing economic outlook can provide the leverage; on the other hand a mistaken perception of the other side on the consequences of coming to a deal may be more difficult to identify but easier to remedy.

The composition of your negotiating team can be something you may or may not have influence over. However, if you are the lead negotiator you should have the right to feel they are under your control while actively engaged in negotiations. This of course is more easily achieved if the ground rules are made clear to them: what their job is and what you expect from them – even in the simplest of negotiations.

The 'culture' of industrial relations in any particular workplace or company can influence the form negotiations will take. Where the 'new culture' of human resource management with Total Quality Management and participative workforces exists, the form of negotiations may lean towards being integrative and joint problem solving. In other environments the likely form of negotiations may be less predictable. In whatever form, a different approach is required and preparation made to meet it.

In grievance handling involving personal cases, greater opportunities exist to shape expected outcomes. However, preparation is no less important and can be even more crucial.

Personal cases usually mean there is something personal at stake in which pride can be a significant factor. That being the case, individuals normally, and quite reasonably, explain their side of events. However, this usually does not, at first anyway, explain fully the circumstances or the cause, meaning that there is an equally plausible but contradictory version around somewhere. In these circumstances, listening and questioning has to be more forensic while maintaining empathy in your approach. Overlying this aspect, of course, are a negotiator's obligations in relation to equality and discriminatory behaviour. The harassed and harasser need to be treated differently once a *prima facie* case has been determined.

Deciding your negotiating objectives and priorities before you start any serious negotiations is the only real way of measuring how much progress you are making. You do not need the Negotiator's Aspirations Matrix in every negotiation but you may find it a useful method of anticipating the other side and sorting out a deal with your own team.

You will have recognised that the face-to-face phase of the negotiations is the most intense part of the process, but substantially relies on what you did beforehand and how you deploy that now. It is at this stage that the combination of your power position, your arguments, and skills in deploying them and responding to the other side come together. Controlling your emotions and behaviour in the interests of reaching your objective is of key importance. Provocative outbursts may impress the uninitiated in the gallery, but not a skilful opponent. Getting fluidity going, smoking-out an offer, can require you to probe the other side's position by a questioning process that can be anything from simple and straightforward to forensic. Don't simply attack impediments to progress, unblock them.

Offers can frequently be elusive, masked, shielded by doubts or conditions. They therefore need fleshing out by questions, combined with encouragement and reassurance if that is required. Deciding on when the 'final offer' has been reached involves a skilled judgement, but very often the behaviour and mood of the other side or your own tells you when you have reached that point.

Although it is important that you remain positive and assured of reaching a settlement, sometimes no deal is better than the one on offer. You must, therefore, have in the back of your mind a strategy for dealing with a failure to reach a deal. Letting time take its course, applying sanctions, seeking conciliation, mediation or arbitration are all useful and legitimate ways of reaching out for a deal.

The tactical use of the law as a form of pressure or as a sanction very much depends on how much law you think you have in your favour. But it has its place, at the appropriate time and in certain circumstances, in the tool-box of negotiators. On issues with an equality connotation, negotiators must observe the obligations laid down in the law (see Appendices A and B).

Information technology increasingly encourages negotiators to use that means to communicate. In this book I have tried to encourage you to use whatever means assist your purpose. However, you do have to be aware of the drawbacks as well as the advantages and adjust your skills accordingly.

This book has essentially been aimed at negotiators in the workplace. It set out to unravel what is sometimes regarded as the dark art of negotiations. As such it has relevance to anyone studying the subject area. The pressures negotiators are under and the complexity of the environment they operate in are a worldwide condition. I hope this book in some small way assists you in your task.

Further Reading

Richard E. Walton and Robert B. McKersie, *A Behavioural Theory of Labour Negotiations* (McGraw Hill, 1965). This is a profound academic study of negotiations with American examples.

Samfrits Le Poole, *Never Take No For An Answer* (Kogan Page, 1991). This is a guide to successful negotiations and contains practical insights and real-life examples.

John Benson, Gavin Kennedy and John McMillan, *Managing Negotiations* (Hutchinson Books, 1987). This book is in its third edition and is essentially aimed at managers. It includes the authors' eight-step approach.

Alan Fowler, *Negotiations – Skills and Strategies* (Institute of Personnel Management, 1990) – a practitioner's book.

Appendix A

Extract from the UK Equal Opportunities Commission's Code of Practice for the Elimination of Discrimination in Employment

INTRODUCTION

1. The UK EOC issues this Code of Practice for the following purposes:

(a) for the elimination of discrimination in employment;
(b) to give guidance as to what steps it is reasonably practicable for employers to take to ensure that their employees do not in the course of their employment act unlawfully contrary to the Sex Discrimination Act (SDA);
(c) for the promotion of equality of opportunity between men and women in employment.

The SDA prohibits discrimination against men, as well as against women. It also requires that married people should not be treated less favourably than single people of the same sex.

It should be noted that the provisions of the SDA – and therefore of this Code – apply to the UK-based subsidiaries of foreign companies.

2. The Code gives guidance to employers, trade unions and employment agencies on measures which can be taken to achieve equality. The chances of success of any organisation will clearly be improved if it seeks to develop the abilities of all employees, and the Code shows the close link which exists between equal opportunity and good employment practice. In some cases, an initial cost may be involved, but this should be more than compensated for by better relationships and better use of human resources.

EMPLOYERS' RESPONSIBILITY

4. The primary responsibility at law rests with each employer to ensure that there is no unlawful discrimination. It is important, however, that measures to eliminate discrimination or promote equality of opportunity should be understood and supported by all employees. Employers are therefore recommended to involve their employees in equal opportunity policies.

INDIVIDUAL EMPLOYEES' RESPONSIBILITY

5. While the main responsibility for eliminating discrimination and providing equal opportunity is that of the employer, individual employees at all levels have responsibilities too. They must not discriminate or knowingly aid the employer to do so.

TRADE UNION RESPONSIBILITY

6. The full commitment of trade unions is essential for the elimination of discrimination and for the successful operation of an equal opportunities policy. Much can be achieved by collective bargaining and throughout the Code it is assumed that all the normal procedures will be followed.

7. It is recommended that unions should co-operate in the introduction and implementation of equal opportunity policies where employers have decided to introduce them, and should urge that such policies be adopted where they have not yet been introduced.

8. Trade unions have a responsibility to ensure that their representatives and members do not unlawfully discriminate on grounds of sex or marriage in the admission or treatment of members. The guidance in this Code also applies to trade unions in their role as employers.

Appendix B

Extract from the UK Commission for Racial Equality's Code of Practice

INTRODUCTION: PURPOSE AND STATUS OF THE CODE

This Code aims to give practical guidance which will help employers, trade unions, employment agencies and employees to understand not only the provisions of the Race Relations Act and their implications, but also how best they can implement policies to eliminate racial discrimination and to enhance equality of opportunity.

The Code does not impose any legal obligations itself, nor is it an authoritative statement of the law – that can only be provided by the courts and tribunals. If, however, its recommendations are not observed this may result in breaches of the law where the act or omission falls within any of the specific prohibitions of the Act. Moreover its provisions are admissible in evidence in any proceedings under the Race Relations Act before an Industrial Tribunal and if any provision appears to the Tribunal to be relevant to a question arising in the proceedings it must be taken into account in determining that question. If employers take the steps that are set out in the Code to prevent their employees from doing acts of unlawful discrimination they may avoid liability for such acts in any legal proceedings brought against them.

Employees of all racial groups have a right to equal opportunity. Employers ought to provide it. To do so is likely to involve some expenditure, at least in staff time and effort. But if a coherent and effective programme of equal opportunity is developed it will help industry to make full use of the abilities of its entire workforce. It is therefore particularly important for all those concerned – employers, trade unions and employees alike – to co-operate with goodwill in adopting and giving effect to measures for securing such equality. We welcome the commitment already made by the CBI and TUC to the principle of equal opportunity. The TUC has recommended a model equal opportunity clause for inclusion in collective agreements and the CBI has published a statement favouring the application by companies of constructive equal opportunity policies.

A concerted policy to eliminate both race and sex discrimination often provides the best approach. Guidance on equal opportunity between men and women is the responsibility of the Equal Opportunities Commission.

PART 1: THE RESPONSIBILITIES OF EMPLOYERS

1.1 Responsibility for providing equal opportunity for all job applicants and employees rests primarily with employers. To this end it is recommended that they should adopt, implement and monitor an equal opportunity policy to ensure that there is no unlawful discrimination and that equal opportunity is genuinely available.

1.2 This policy should be clearly communicated to all employees – e.g. through notice boards, circulars, contracts of employment or written notifications to individual employees.

Equal Opportunity Policies

1.3 An equal opportunity policy aims to ensure:

(a) that no job applicant or employee receives less favourable treatment than another on racial grounds;

(b) that no applicant or employee is placed at a disadvantage by requirements or conditions which have a disproportionately adverse effect on his or her racial group and which cannot be shown to be justifiable on other than racial grounds;

(c) that, where appropriate and where permissible under the Race Relations Act, employees of under-represented racial groups are given training and encouragement to achieve equal opportunity within the organisation.

PART 2: THE RESPONSIBILITIES OF INDIVIDUAL EMPLOYEES

2.1 While the primary responsibility for providing equal opportunity rests with the employer, individual employees at all levels and of all racial groups have responsibilities too. Good race relations depend on them as much as on management, and so their attitudes and activities are very important.

2.2 The following actions by individual employees would be unlawful:

(a) discrimination in the course of their employment against fellow employees or job applicants on racial grounds, for example, in selection decisions for recruitment, promotion, transfer and training;

(b) inducing, or attempting to induce other employees, unions or management to practice unlawful discrimination. For example, they should not refuse to accept other employees from particular racial groups;

(c) victimising individuals who have made allegations or complaints of racial discrimination or provided information about such discrimination.

2.3 To assist in preventing racial discrimination and promoting equal opportunity it is recommended that individual employees should:

(a) co-operate in measures introduced by management designed to ensure equal opportunity and non-discrimination;

(b) where such measures have not been introduced, press for their introduction (through their trade union where appropriate);

(c) draw the attention of management and, where appropriate, their trade unions to suspected discriminatory acts or practices;

(d) refrain from harassment or intimidation of other employees on racial grounds, for example, by attempting to discourage them from continuing employment. Such action may be unlawful if it is taken by employees against those subject to their authority.

PART 3: THE RESPONSIBILITIES OF TRADE UNIONS

3.1 Trade unions, in common with a number of other organisations, have a dual role as employers and providers of services specifically covered by the Race Relations Act.

3.2 In their role as employer, unions have the responsibilities set out in Part 1 of the Code. They also have a responsibility to ensure that their representatives and members do not discriminate against any particular racial group in the admission or treatment of members, or as colleagues, supervisors or subordinates.

3.3 In addition, trade union officials at national and local level and shopfloor representatives at plant level have an important part to play on behalf of their members in preventing unlawful discrimination and in promoting equal opportunity and good race relations. Trade unions should encourage and press for equal opportunity policies so that measures to prevent discrimination at the workplace can be introduced with the clear commitment of both management and unions.

Admission of Members

3.4 It is unlawful for trade unions to discriminate on racial grounds:

(a) by refusing membership;
(b) by offering less favourable terms of membership.

Treatment of Members

3.5 It is unlawful for trade unions to discriminate on racial grounds against existing members:

(a) by varying their terms of membership, depriving them of membership or subjecting them to any other detriment;

(b) by treating them less favourably in the benefits, facilities or services provided. They may include:

training facilities
welfare and insurance schemes

entertainment and social events
processing of grievances
negotiations
assistance in disciplinary or dismissal procedures.

3.6 In addition, it is recommended that unions ensure that in cases where members of particular racial groups believe that they are suffering racial discrimination, whether by the employer or the union itself, serious attention is paid to the reasons for this belief and that any discrimination which may be occurring is stopped.

Disciplining Members who Discriminate

3.7 It is recommended that deliberate acts of unlawful discrimination by union members are treated as disciplinary offences.

Positive Action

3.8 Although they are not legally required, positive measures are allowed by the law to encourage and provide training for members of particular racial groups which have been under-represented in trade union membership or in trade union posts. (Discrimination at the point of selection, however, is not permissible in these circumstances.)
   3.9 It is recommended that, wherever appropriate and reasonably practicable, trade unions should:

   (a) encourage individuals from these groups to join the union. Where appropriate, recruitment material should be translated into other languages;
   (b) encourage individuals from these groups to apply for union posts and provide training to help fit them for such posts.

Training and Information

3.10 Training and information play a major part in the avoidance of discrimination and the promotion of equal opportunity. It is recommended that trade unions should:

(a) provide training and information for officers, shop stewards and representatives on their responsibilities for equal opportunity. This training and information should cover

- the Race Relations Act and the nature and causes of discrimination;
- the backgrounds of racial minority groups and communication needs;
- the effects of prejudice;
- equal opportunity policies;
- avoiding discrimination when representing members;

(b) ensure that members and representatives, whatever their racial group, are informed of their role in the union, and of industrial relations and union procedures and structures. This may be done, for example:

- through translation of material;
- through encouragement to participate in industrial relations courses and industrial language training.

Pressure to Discriminate

3.11 It is unlawful for trade union members or representatives to induce or to attempt to induce those responsible for employment decisions to discriminate:

(a) in the recruitment, promotion, transfer, training or dismissal of employees;
(b) in terms of employment, benefits, facilities or services.

3.12 For example, they should not:

(a) restrict the numbers of a particular racial group in a section, grade or department;
(b) resist changes designed to remove indirect discrimination, such as those in craft apprentice schemes, or in agreements concerning seniority rights or mobility between departments.

Victimisation

3.13 It is unlawful to victimise individuals who have made allegations or complaints of racial discrimination or provided information about such discrimination.

Avoidance of Discrimination

3.14 Where unions are involved in selection decisions for recruitment, promotion, training or transfer, for example through recommendation or veto, it is unlawful for them to discriminate on racial grounds.

3.15 It is recommended that they should instruct their members accordingly and examine their procedures and joint agreements to ensure that they do not contain indirectly discriminatory requirements or conditions, such as:

- unjustifiable restrictions on transfers between departments or irrelevant and unjustifiable selection criteria which have a disproportionately adverse effect on particular racial groups.

Union Involvement in Equal Opportunity Policies

3.16 It is recommended that:

(a) unions should co-operate in the introduction and implementation of full equal opportunity policies;

(b) unions should negotiate the adoption of such policies where they have not been introduced or the extension of existing policies where these are too narrow;

(c) unions should co-operate with measures to monitor the progress of equal opportunity policies, or encourage management to introduce them where they do not already exist. Where appropriate this may be done through analysis of the distribution of employees and job applicants according to ethnic origin;

(d) where monitoring shows that discrimination has occurred or is occurring, unions should co-operate in measures to eliminate it;

(e) although positive action is not legally required, unions should encourage management to take such action where there is under-representation of particular racial groups in particular jobs, and where management itself introduces positive action representatives should support it;

(f) similarly, where there are communications difficulties, management should be asked to take whatever action is appropriate to overcome them.

For fuller information on discrimination and equal opportunity in employment or detailed information on a specific aspect which has relevance to you in negotiations, you should consult the full versions of the Codes of Practice on Race and Sex Discrimination et al and/or the UK Race Relations Act (1976) or the Sex Discrimination Act (1975) and relevant case law.

Index

accommodation *see* venue
accuracy
   in written correspondence,
     139
   see also written notes
adjournments, use of, 59,
    109–10, 122, 136
adversarial negotiations, 2,
    8–9
   closing negotiations on,
     116–20
   preparation for, 65, 66
Advisory, Conciliation and
    Arbitration Service
    (ACAS), 30, 124, 144
agenda
   contentious, 94–5
   multi-item claims, 72–3,
    76, 92
   parallel approach to, 93
   sequential approach to,
    93–4
   single item claims, 92
   see also objectives
aggression
   and telephone
    negotiations, 137–8, 140
   in written correspondence,
    139, 141
agreement
   drafting of, 128–9
   editing the infrastructure,
    127–9
   implementation of, 130–1
   misunderstandings at
    editing stage, 129–30

options in event of failure,
    122–5, 155
premature, 100, 119
ratification of, 130
see also offers
alcohol, 135
anticipation, and counter-
    responses, 68–9, 76–7
arbitration
   ACAS, 30, 144
   pendulum, 125
   traditional, 125
argument
   dealing with weaknesses in,
    90
   power of, 46
   presentation of, 90–1
   use of, to reach negotiating
    position, 54–6
Aspirations Matrix,
    Negotiator's, **74–5**, 76,
    77, 154
   use of in childcare
    agreement, 77, **78**, 79,
    80, 81, **82**, 83
assumptions, testing, 68
attitudes, 11, 152
   of management, 12–16, 17
   negotiator's, 18, 19, 20, 22,
    96–7
authority *see* legitimacy

ballots, on sanctions, 123
beliefs, as factor, 13, 18–19
bluff, use of, 48, 117, 126
British Coal, and NUM, 52–3,
    123–4

167

Index by Auriol Griffith-Jones